TO THE RESCUE

HOW IMMIGRANTS SAVED THE AMERICAN FILM INDUSTRY

1896 - 1912

KEN WEISS

TO THE RESCUE

HOW IMMIGRANTS SAVED THE AMERICAN FILM INDUSTRY

1896 - 1912

KEN WEISS

Austin & Winfield, Publishers
San Francisco - London - Bethesda
1997

Library of Congress Cataloging-in-Publication Data

Weiss, Ken
    To the rescue : how immigrants saved the American film industry
    1896-1912 / Ken Weiss.
      p. cm.
    Includes bibliographical references and index.
    ISBN 1-57292-051-3 (cloth : alk. paper). -- ISBN 1-57292-050-5 (pbk. :
    alk. paper)
    1. Motion pictures—United States—History. 2. Immigrants—United
    States. 3. Motion pictures—Social aspects—United States.
    4. Motion pictures—Economic aspects—United States. I. Title.
    PN1993.5.U6W42   1996
    384'.8'0973'09041—dc21   96-46971
                                                CIP

Editorial Inquiries:
Austin & Winfield, Publishers
7831 Woodmont Avenue, #345
Bethesda, MD 20814
(301) 654-7335

To Order: (800) 99-AUSTIN

ACKNOWLEDGEMENTS

This book would not have been possible without the efforts of the many scholars before me whose studies are cited shamelessly throughout the text. This project began as a Ph. D dissertation and I must single out the late Dr. Sidney Aronson for the crucial inspiration and guidance he provided. The New York Public Library's Theater Collection at the Lincoln Center of Performing Arts, as well as the research rooms of the 42nd Street Library, the Museum of the City of New York Photograph Department and the Northampton (Massachusetts) Public Library provided invaluable assistance. The always-helpful staff of the Museum of Modern Art Library and Film Studies Department offered historical resources not readily available elsewhere. The Torrington (Connecticut) Public Library and the Dayton (Ohio) Public Library offered timely information.

I am also indebted to the many people who were willing to share their earliest experiences with me, in taped interviews. Members of the Society of Cinephiles provided generous and informative contributions.

CONTENTS

INTRODUCTION

It is no surprise that the working class was important to the early film industry. But rescuing it? That's another story. However, it is what I believe happened, and this book presents much of the evidence that led me to this conclusion. What I've examined is a particular, brief period in the early development of motion pictures in the United States, an era that predated any institutional structure--for example, there was no such thing as a movie theater, and early movie audiences were unconsciously experimenting with the social space of the theater and improvising their relationship with it before the medium's rules of spectatorship had evolved.

It is my contention that, during this relatively anarchic period between 1906 and 1912, as a result of a number of social forces discussed in detail later, the newly arrived immigrant population, as part of a larger working-class audience (usually individually and collectively marginal), wielded an influence over movie program content and method of presentation totally incommensurate with its actual status and number in society. This despite the fact that moving pictures had been developed for and introduced to the middle class. We will find that in certain instances immigrant preferences determined to a large degree not just the content and subject matter of many films within a given theater, but their ultimate availability to other segments of the movie audience as well. Immigrants entered the picture at a critical juncture for the developing industry, as it was languishing among its initial, elite audience.

I suggest that the working-class audience not only appropriated the presentational space signified by the neighborhood theater and utilized that space for its own social needs, but also that the tastes and, to an extent, the mere presence of the immigrant audience represented a perceived threat to the exhibitors' desire and ability to cater to the much prized middle-class audience. Further, I propose that for approximately six years these tastes strongly influenced and retarded middle-class acceptance of moving pictures. Implicit within this dynamic is the premise that different

1

neighborhoods did indeed demonstrate preferences, and that individual theater owners could and did exercise options that would enable them to accommodate the tastes of their particular audience.

Reduced to their most essential forms, the questions are: did working-class people actually appropriate the neighborhood nickelodeons, did they strongly influence the content and method of presentation of moving pictures? Did they retard middle-class acceptance of moving pictures? And, finally, did they really "rescue" the American moving picture industry? I'm inclined to answer "yes" to all four questions, and this book will explain why.

It's appropriate to point out what will become obvious--the anecdotal nature of much of the data. The material may or may not support or provide evidence of specific points of view, but considerably more data are required before answers can be declared conclusive. However, given the area under study and the scarcity of primary source material regarding attendance at moving picture theaters by age, religion, ethnicity and gender, social facts will only be acquired by massive collection and imbrication of just such anecdotal data. These data have allowed me to make certain assumptions, but no more than that.

It is evident that, in many immigrant and working-class neighborhoods, the local movie theater functioned as an extension of the community, a place in which the immigrant could feel at home. This may have been troublesome to the entrepreneurs who controlled the production of films and the ownership of movie technology, and even more so to the exhibitors and theater owners who dealt directly with this undisciplined patronage. While catering to the immigrant audience was profitable, it was also limiting. Many of the theater owners, like William Fox, were themselves recent escapees from the ghetto and aspired to middle-class values. Middle-class patrons were reluctant to attend moving picture theaters for a number of reasons (to be discussed later), but were particularly leery of theaters that admitted working-class, immigrant patrons. Immigrants smelled bad and were unruly, as contemporary accounts often remind us. Further, the kinds of films they apparently required--short, action-filled and easy to understand--were least appealing to middle-class audiences.

Social life in these storefront theaters, boisterous, familiar and participative, was a far cry from the silent, isolated experience that was later developed and enforced. How the manufacturers (as they called themselves) of films eventually expanded their market, recaptured the middle-class and simultaneously minimized the influence of the lower-class audience while standardizing reception, is part of the story to unfold.

Among film-study theorists and historians, there is considerable and growing interest in audience-reception studies, with the recognition that audiences are more than just paying customers. Historian Harold Stadler has written that, in traditional film theories, "the viewer's part is taken for granted, but is never seriously investigated." Theorist Janet Staiger has stated "...propositions forwarded by philosophers of the ontology, epistemology and effectivity of moving images need to be tested by confrontation with historical spectators." Researcher Bruce Austin has noted that while the commercial and technological development of the medium are all well known, "...the medium's audience is, at best, a fuzzy soft-focus image..."[1] Most current reception studies concentrate on how the viewer interprets or "reads" the film, and on the nature of this process, through analysis of signs and symbols. Communication theory, with its emphasis on audience perception, provides theoretical validation to this line of research. Joyce E. Jesionowski, a film theorist, has noted

> Film theory is beginning to recognize that the film experience is some kind of contract between the filmmaker, who constitutes meaningful signs in a film, and the viewer, who "decodes" these signs immediately during the film, or later, upon reflection.[2]

Film curator Eileen Bowser, of the Museum of Modern Art, noted a 1914 interview with J. Searle Dawley, a director who had started with Edison but moved up to Famous Players. Dawley anticipated communication theory (and Eisenstein's montage theory) when he stated that in film an actor, doing little more than standing motionless and "gazing into a lighted window," could nonetheless "convey to the mind all the depths of love and hate." Further,

> his position is carried to the spectator by what has gone before or by what may come afterwards.... It is the sequence of movement and scenes that is the essence of this new art....each auditor is creating his own emotions and language for the characters before him....and they are according to his own mental and spiritual standard. Therefore, the spectator is supplying the thoughts and words of the actor and becomes a part of the performance itself.[3]

Communication theory emphasizes that only the receiver (viewer) can actually assign meaning.[4] While the filmmaker supplies the signs and symbols through which he or she *intends* meaning, these symbols can only be assigned meaning by the viewer. If one accepts this, it becomes clear that the semiotic messages in a film

3

or theatrical ambiance can be interpreted selectively by individuals and groups, and that each can arrive at different conclusions regarding "meaning." Because such factors as culture, religion and economic status are major influences in forming attitudes and perceptions, one can assume that these differences between, say, the middle-class and the working-class, strongly affected the way these two audiences would receive and react to the new medium, including its surroundings. This study concentrates on the behavior of members of the audience and their observable or stated reactions, particularly in relation to one another, and the ways by which behavior may have influenced the content and exhibition of moving pictures. As we shall see, class difference is at the heart of this study.

The development of moving pictures appears to have followed the cycle of media progression referred to as the Elitist-Popular-Specialized (EPS) cycle, a concept developed in 1971 by mass-communication scholars John Merrill and Ralph Lowenstein. In *Media Messages and Men*, Merrill and Lowenstein (apparently assuming the introduction of such media in capitalist economic systems) were the first to point out that all mass media develop in three stages. The first is the Elitist stage, during which the medium is consumed by the affluent members of the society. The second, or Popular stage, sees the medium embraced by the working class, while in the third, Specialized stage, the medium is segmented to appeal to specialized markets. The notion of the medium as "high culture" usually emerges during the first stage, and sometimes "trickles down" to the masses, while the medium consumed by the working class in the second stage becomes identified as "popular culture."[5]

This is of interest here largely because moving pictures seem to have flaunted some of these rules. There is considerable evidence of "trickle up" in movie development, and there has been much debate among sociologists as to what signifies high and low culture in regard to film--and whether film can be considered high culture at all. Bernard Rosenberg has stated that the defining process is time-specific, and that "The judgment of one generation is merely a fragment of the consensus of many generations, one vote in the parliament of history." Rosenberg asks, "By what right do we call high culture 'high'?"[6] The question has been argued vigorously for decades. Ernest van den Haag believed that high culture trickles down from above, in that some forms of culture, like certain art, legitimate theater, classical music and literature were inherently high. David Manning White apparently accepted this view when he signified Paddy Chayevsky's success in

4

going "from television to the legitimate theater of New York."[7] The superiority of the latter over the former is automatically assumed.

The terms themselves invite confusion. Dwight Macdonald pointed out that works of "high culture" are sometimes more popular than the products of "popular culture" products. For Macdonald, mass culture was "imposed from above... fabricated by technicians hired by businessmen." Herbert Gans, while recognizing the destructive aspects of much of mass culture, nonetheless viewed it as expressing the wants of the general public, and noted that all people have the "right to the culture they prefer."[8]

While definitions of high culture change with time--and no claim can be made for permanence, patterns do emerge which challenge trickle-down (EPS) theory in regard to film. For although moving pictures were first conceived as an entertainment for the upper and middle classes, there is little indication that this elite group ever considered it any more than that and least of all, art. A wonder of science, yes. But not art. If any claims for high culture can be made for moving pictures, it is evident that the transition occurred almost wholly within the parameters of a low-culture, mass-market medium. Financed by businessmen, Porter, Griffith and many others were developing the language of film and experimenting with narrative at a time when the audience and principal decoders of these symbols were at least 70 percent working-class and largely first- or second- generation immigrants.

It is ironic that, in contemporary accounts of *Intolerance* (1916), many intellectuals, not being regular movie-goers, were confused by the film's editing techniques. For the most part, however, there was little in *Intolerance* that had not been tried before in one or more of the approximately 450 films Griffith had made for Biograph between 1908 and 1913, and I would claim that the average movie-going immigrant had less difficulty understanding *Intolerance* than many of the intellectuals who had been scrupulously avoiding movies during those years. The movie model seems unique. Unlike jazz, moving pictures can lay no claim to being a folk art, for it was originally a creation of capitalists and the "technicians" Macdonald abhorred, as a commodity for consumption by mass audiences.

I have attempted to locate the advent of moving pictures within its historical period, primarily through the eyes and experiences of the three major participant groups: the producers/ manufacturers of films, the exhibitors and, particularly, the audience, which was the nexus for the social unrest and industry perturbation that were to distinguish the working class years of moving-picture development, and constitute most of this study.

5

I shall present a social history of the medium by dividing its early years into two periods: The period of introduction (1896-1905), during which moving pictures are introduced as middle-class entertainment, and the era of participation (1906-1912), when the working class audience become influential. Each period is studied from the point of view of the participants, who fall into the three aforementioned interdependent groups: the manufacturer/studios that produced the films, the exhibitor/theater owners who presented them, and the audiences who paid to see them. Much of my emphasis will be on the social factors (including economic, moral, health and safety concerns) related to audience behavior, reception and presentation that tended to restrain development of the industry, and on how these problems were mediated.

The research for this study has involved published histories, particularly for the period prior to the development of projected films. I am especially indebted to the rigorous research of Charles Musser, Joseph North and Robert Allen, whose works provided valuable data concerning this early period. The center of my thesis is the working-class audience and its interdependent relationship, the films presented, and the methods of presentation. Most published research has concentrated on the latter two factors: the films (their content, style and production), as well as the studios and the people who acted in and produced them; and the methods of presentation (theaters, "chains," and programs), together with the organizations and people who developed them. My interest was in the nature of the audience, and the ways by which this audience influenced production and presentation. Because of this difference in point of view, I have on occasion used data in ways unintended by their authors. For example, Robert Allen uses the information from his article cited on pages 43-44, to suggest that the significance of the working-class audience was perhaps overestimated, while I use the same data to indicate the opposite.

I have relied most extensively on contemporary sources like newspapers (including local papers, such as the *New Rochelle Pioneer, Hampshire Gazette,* and *Torrington Evening Register)* and trade publications, most notably *Moving Picture World,* which began publication in 1907, presenting trade news on a weekly basis, and reprinting of relevant articles and news culled from newspapers and magazines throughout the country. *Moving Picture World* covered nearly every aspect of production, distribution and exhibition (including letters from theater owners complaining about the films and/or their audiences) and employed writers like Stephen Bush (also a moving-picture "lecturer"), who, almost alone, often reported on the reactions and behavior of the working-class audience.

6

Other trade publications were useful, as were biographies. The published recollections of Edward Wagenknecht, for example, are particularly valued by researchers, not simply because Wagenknecht was contemporaneous with the era but also because of the perspective he offered as a teacher, scholar, author and literary critic. General consumer publications, such as *The Saturday Evening Post* and *The Ladies Home Journal,* provided a middle-class overview of the medium's reception, or non reception in some instances.

The research rooms and divisions of the New York Public Library were, as always, essential and invaluable. The New Rochelle, Torrington, Connecticut, and Northampton, Massachusetts, libraries provided material not found elsewhere. The Museum of Modern Art's film-studies library provided access to industry documents, records and court testimony, as well as the opportunity to screen many of the era's films.

Additionally, I have conducted interviews with seventeen people who were contemporaneous with the era, and I have used quotes from these interviews throughout this study. Interview transcripts and tapes are available to academic researchers upon request. Many of the interviewees turned out to have been from the middle class during the early 1900s. My initial reaction to this was disappointment, because my study involved the urban working class. But, two years later, the interviews were valued precisely because they were so dissimilar to the working class-experience, a viewpoint that led me to suspect an inverse relationship between the social class of children and their attendance at movies, which is also explored within this book.

1. THE PERIOD OF INTRODUCTION (1896-1905)

Edison and the Collaborative Development of the Moving Picture

The common notion regarding the development of motion pictures usually involves immigrant Jews imbued with grit and visionary foresight who created the industry, more or less, and with their bare hands built great empires. For example, the introduction to Neil Gabler's *An Empire of Their Own,* states "that the American film industry...was founded and for more than thirty years operated by Eastern European Jews."[1] Actually, the founders of the industry were for the most part upper- and middle-class Anglo-Saxon inventors, entrepreneurs and businessmen, with scarcely a Jew among them. The idea of creating entertainment was decidedly secondary to most of them. They saw themselves as manufacturers, involved in a new and wondrous branch of science and industry, rather than providers of entertainment. As they were respectable businessmen, in many cases associated with prominent bankers and investors, dignity and propriety were desirable. Their primary intent (as we shall see) was to sell machines. The films that went with them were considered fodder for their machines. Ironically, while enrichment or fame might have been the goal of these men, very few of the original founders achieved lasting success in moving pictures. Although they started the vertical integration of the industry, and initiated what came to be known as the star system, only one of the nine producing companies that are recognized as having started the business was still active after 1918.

Although a number of companies were prominent for brief periods during the first few decades of the medium's growth, one company in particular dominates the first ten years--the Edison Manufacturing Company. The story of Edison is, in addition to technical innovation, one of law suits (Edison was notorious for using law suits like a club to intimidate competitors) and monopolistic ambition, involving in its legalistic web virtually every moving-picture machine and film producer of the day.

When moving pictures were first commercially projected onto a large screen in 1896, photographed movies were already seven years old, though in the form of peep shows. In 1889, Thomas Alva Edison and his staff, as well as others, had begun working on a machine for photographic images that would provide the illusion of motion. Earlier, Edison got the idea for the machine after meeting with photographer Eadweard Muybridge and witnessing the Zoopraxiscope, a projecting machine that displayed the photographer's famous action photographs in a sequence rapid enough to suggest motion, like slides being shown very quickly. Later that year, Edison wrote that he was "experimenting upon an instrument which does for the Eye what the phonograph does for the Ear, which is the recording and reproduction of things in motion." What Edison was imagining was a machine that would be able to show the tiny images (about 42,000 of them) imprinted on a phonograph-type cylinder that would rotate--at 180 images per turn--past a viewing lens. Edison anticipated that a viewer, peering through a microscope, would listen to sound from a phonograph while watching nearly a half hour of moving pictures.[2]

Thus inspired, Edison turned the details of development over to his associates, particularly William Kennedy Laurie Dickson. An important contributor to early film development, Dickson was a Brittany-born Englishman who had once written an impassioned letter to Edison pleading for a job--and had been turned down. He emigrated to America in 1881 and, after determined efforts managed to get a job in Edison's Testing and Experimental Department on Goerck Street in New York City. Dickson was soon managing the department; he had also become Edison's "official" photographer, which made him valuable when Edison's motion-picture project was initiated.[3]

Work with moving pictures, despite some tentative progress, was slow. Edison was preoccupied with a magnetic ore-milling device for separating iron from earth, whose potential seemed much more impressive; much of his and Dickson's time was spent (fruitlessly, as it turned out) on that project. In 1890 Dickson returned to the development of what came to be known as the Kinetoscope; with an assistant, William Heise, he designed a different kind of camera, one that used strips of film. This had been suggested by Edison, who had picked up the idea from a French inventor, Etienne Jules Marey, whom he had met in Europe. "I knew instantly that Marey had the right idea," Edison said.[4]

Within a year Edison was showing a Kinetoscope "peep-hole" viewing machine to visitors from the National Federation of Women's Clubs, who were impressed by "a most marvelous picture. It bowed and smiled and waved its hands and took off its hat with the most perfect naturalness and grace. Every motion was perfect." "It" was Dickson. Patent applications for the new moving-picture camera (Kinetograph) and viewing device (Kinetoscope) were submitted to the United States Patent Office on August 24, 1891.[5] Edison was not particularly optimistic regarding the future of moving pictures, being convinced, as were most observers, that at best they would be an interesting fad, but not much more. Accordingly, he did not bother to file for European patent protection for the Kinetograph.[6]

Until now, the films displayed were shot around the Edison plant--Dickson gesturing, an employee smoking a pipe, a man juggling, etc. In order to provide more suitable films for his machines, especially in view of their upcoming exhibition at the World's Columbian Exposition, Edison had a studio built next to his laboratory in West Orange, New Jersey. Dickson, the designer, called it "The Kinetographic Theater." The workers themselves called it the "Black Maria," because it reminded them of the black arrest wagons used by the police, and that was the name that endured. The structure, completed in February, 1893, was about fifty feet long and thirteen feet wide, with black tarpaper-lined interiors and exteriors. Hinged segments of its roof could be lifted to allow sunlight to fall inside and the entire structure could be rotated on tracks to follow the sun.[7]

On May 9, members of the Department of Physics of the Brooklyn Institute of Arts and Sciences examined a Kinetoscope. George M. Hopkins, president of the department, after giving due credit to those inventors who had preceded Edison in this line of interest, provided an introductory description of how the machine worked.

> There are 700 impressions on each strip, and when these pictures are shown in succession in the kinetograph the light is intercepted 700 times during one revolution of the strip. The duration of each image is one-ninety-second of a second, and the entire strip passes through the instrument in about thirty seconds. In the Kinetograph each image dwells upon the retina until it is replaced by the succeeding one, and the difference between any picture and the preceding one is so slight as to render it impossible to observe the intermittent character of the picture.[8]

Early in 1894, as the Columbian Exposition drew to a close, twenty-five Kinetoscopes were sold to Frank Gammon (who had been secretary of the Awards Committee of the Exposition) and Alfred O. Tate. Most of the peep-hole machines were for viewing only, but a few were "Kinetophones," which realized Edison's original intent by providing an accompanying phonograph, which played cylinder records so the viewer could enjoy music while watching moving pictures. Of the twenty-five Kinetoscopes, ten were assigned to an arcade at 1155 Broadway, near Herald Square, which became New York City's first moving-picture arcade, grossing $120 on opening day, April 14, 1894, and $16,171.56 in its first year--a goodly sum at the time. The films exhibited on this occasion included *Highland Dance* (a young couple in full costume), *Organ Grinder,* and *Trained Bears*, tame general interest subjects suitable for the middle-class men and women who would be paying five cents to see each film, lasting about thirty seconds. Of the remaining Kinetoscopes, five were shipped to Atlantic City, New Jersey, and ten to Chicago.[9]

Obviously, the early development of motion pictures, rather than being the product of any one person's genius, was an amalgamation of ideas from a number of people. The sometimes haphazard and increasingly collaborative nature of moving-picture development is illustrated not only by Marey's sharing of information with Edison, but by the experience of the Latham family. Of old Virginia aristocracy, down on their luck and in 1894 living in New York, the Lathams were alert to commercial possibilities and ordered several Kinetoscopes.

Suspecting that increased running time would enable them to show prize fights, they worked with Edison to expand Kinetograph film capacity from 50 feet to 150 feet, while reducing camera speed from about forty frames per second to thirty. This enabled them to show abbreviated rounds that lasted a little more than a minute. They contracted with two boxers, Michael Leonard ("the Beau Brummel of the prize ring") and the lightweight contender, Jack Cushing, to stage a ten-round fight, which was filmed at the Black Maria in July, 1894. The world's first prize fight film ended when Cushing was knocked out in the sixth round. The Lathams, with some partners, opened a Kinetoscope parlor in August, at 83 Nassau Street in downtown New York. Six Kinetoscopes were installed, each containing a round of the Cushing-Leonard fight. It was an immediate hit. Within days, lines of waiting viewers trailed into the street and police were required to keep order.[10] Boxing quickly became one of the most popular of all Kinetoscope subjects.

In 1894, when Kinetoscope sales were showing signs of becoming big business, the Edison Manufacturing Company named associates Norman C. Raff and Frank R. Gammon to head a consortium with exclusive rights to sell Kinetoscopes in the United States and Canada. But that year, which produced Kinetoscope profits of more than $89,000 for the Edison Company, turned out to be the high-water year.

Sales fell in 1895, and Edison's Kinetoscope profits dropped to little more than $4000.[11] Up to this time the Edison Company had borne the costs of film production, but now was no longer willing to do so. Instead, costs were to be shared by those selling the machines; Raff and Gammon, who handled domestic sales, and two other groups with whom Edison had agreements, the aforementioned Latham Kinetoscope Exhibition Company, and the Maguire & Baucus-Continental Commerce Company, which handled international sales.[12]

Part of the problems Edison was experiencing with sales could be traced to his former employee, Dickson. In April, 1895, Dickson, who for some time had been working on motion picture devices with two acquaintances, Henry Norton Marvin and Henry Casler, quit Edison to devote more time to this independent effort. His two partners were the founders of Marvin & Casler, of Canosta, New York, a machine manufactory that had done work for Edison. Dickson, Marvin and Casler were busy developing the Mutoscope, a hand-cranked "book of cards" viewing machine. Instead of utilizing film strips, the Mutoscope displayed photographs as they were flipped very rapidly, one by one, to produce the illusion of movement. A businessman, E. B. Koopman, was the financier of the group.[13]

At first the Koopman-Marvin-Casler-Dickson (K.M.C.D.) group had hoped they could use Edison's Kinetoscope negatives to produce the photograph prints they needed, but Edison refused. So they set about developing a camera of their own.[14] The Mutoscope machines, with their large photographs, were soon more popular than Kinetoscopes, which explained in part why Edison, Raff and Gammon were experiencing sales difficulties. The Mutoscope machines were popular penny-arcade attractions for well over fifty years; when the first Disneyland opened in Anaheim, California in 1955, a featured attraction in the Penny Arcade exhibition on Main Street, was a double row of authentic hand-cranked Mutoscopes.[15]

Kinetoscope viewing, at five cents per one-minute film, was relatively expensive at a time when the average weekly wage was twelve dollars for a sixty-hour week. For comparison, bread cost two or three cents per pound, a quart of milk cost four cents, and a three-course meal of soup, a main dish (with choice of vegetables) and dessert, cost fifteen cents.[16] Kinetoscope parlors, located primarily in metropolitan business and commercial districts throughout the country, catered to a dominantly male middle-class audience that was able to pay the price. In the bout between James J. ("Gentleman Jim") Corbett-Peter Courtney, which was fought in 1894 at the Edison studio in Orange, New Jersey, Courtney was knocked out in the sixth round. It would have cost a Kinetoscope patron thirty cents to watch the fight in its entirety, a discretionary sum not within the reach of working-class laborers.

At their inception, most Kinetoscope parlors were models of Victorian propriety, and represented a significant investment by their owners. A photograph of one such parlor, The Automatic One-Cent Vaudeville, at 48 East 14 Street, reveals an immaculate arcade, its diamond-patterned tile floor glistening under electric lights (another recent wonder), its more than fifty-foot length lined on both sides by Kinetoscope and other amusement machines.[17]

The Automatic One-Cent Vaudeville amusement parlor, about 1904. Projected movies had been in operation for eight years, and peep-show prices had fallen accordingly.

A patron would put a coin into a Kinetoscope machine and peer into a small glass window through which various events could be seen. Each scene or event lasted about twenty seconds. (Before the introduction of a coin-operated mechanism, well-dressed attendants would start machines manually.) The scene might be one of a busy avenue, Annie Oakley shooting at clay targets, Sandow the strong man displaying his muscles, or "Madame Rita" dancing. The attraction was not necessarily the content, but the mere fact that photographs were *moving* in an apparently authentic, lifelike fashion. The most popular subject was boxing; for certain events, such as the heavyweight bout between Corbett and Courtney, fans would move from one machine to another to view successive rounds.[18]

The chief drawback of the Kinetoscope was that it allowed only one viewer at a time to see a performance, and was therefore capital intensive. Parlor operators paid approximately $300 for each Kinetoscope, which required more than 6000 paying viewers before the machine could be considered profitable.[19] The desire was for a means of exhibition that would permit large numbers of people to view a single performance.

The Race for a Projection System

With Kinetoscope sales in decline, Raff and Gammon sought the development of a "projecting Kinetoscope," a machine that would project moving pictures onto a surface so that more than one person at a time could see them. With that end in mind, they formed the Vitascope Company in January, 1896. Soon they would be mediating the development of the projecting apparatus between the various inventors, particularly Thomas Armat and his associate, T. Cushing Daniel, and the Edison organization. Edison had doubts about projected moving pictures, fearing that with so many people able to watch a single film, profits would be reduced. According to Ramsaye, Edison felt that "If we put out a screen machine there will be use for maybe about ten of them in the whole United States...Let's not kill the goose that lays the golden eggs."[20] Frederick A. Anthony, a broker involved in the movie business at that time, later testified:

> I talked with him [Edison] about his patent, and he told me that he didn't think there was a very great future for the moving picture business, and that it was just a fad, and therefore that it would not last very long...[21]

Cooperation among the inventors was essential because they knew that, in the United States and Europe, the development of other moving-picture projection systems was well under way. In 1888, when Edison was first thinking about the Kinetoscope, Louis Augustin Le Prince, a Frenchman, had patented machines that photographed and projected moving pictures. An Englishman, William Friese-Greene, patented a combination camera-projector in 1893. In the United States, one of the first systems to be publicly displayed was the Latham Pantoptikan (from the Latham family, who had turned their attention to projected images), which was exhibited on May 20, 1895, at 153 Broadway, New York. While appreciated for its novelty, the quality of the picture was not satisfactory.[22]

In France, two brothers, Auguste Marie and Louis Jean Lumiére, having studied Edison's Kinetoscope and Kinetograph, devised their own machine, the Cinématographe, in 1895. They shot several films and, on March 22, exhibited them to members of the Society for the Encouragement of National Industry. The Lumiéres, like Edison, did not have much faith in the future of moving pictures and were in no hurry to demonstrate their invention. They offered their first commercial exhibition to a paying public on December 28, 1885, utilizing a basement room of the Grand Cafe in Paris as a theater. A few months later the Lumiéres crossed the Channel and, on February 29, offered England's first public demonstration of motion pictures at Marlborough Hall, London. At about the same time in Berlin, Max and Emil Skladanowsky demonstrated their own camera and projector, called the Bioscope.[23]

In the United States, the K.M.C.D. group, encouraged by the success of their Mutoscope machines, had been reorganized as the American Mutoscope Company, at 841 Broadway, in New York City, and continued work on its own projecting machine, the Biograph. In the United States, Thomas Armat, a Washington, D.C. realtor who had turned inventor after being fascinated by the Anschutz Tachyscope he had seen at the Columbian Exposition, was experimenting with his own projecting machine, the Phantascope. He had noticed that film ran more smoothly if a small loop was employed to reduce film tension, and contrived a sprocket which produced the loop.[24]

In view of all this activity, Edison's efforts were not producing results quickly enough for Raff and Gammon, whose Kinetoscope business had all but collapsed; with growing anxiety they were looking into other projecting-machine systems. When Gammon was given a personal demonstration of Armat's projector, Raff and Gammon decided to back Armat and convinced the Edison Company to manufacture Armat's projector as the Vitascope--under Edison's name to take advantage of the famous inventor's reputation.[25] By this time Edison was aware of the competition, as each interest raced to complete a commercially acceptable projector. The sense of urgency increased when Raff and Gammon heard that several New York vaudeville managers were trying to arrange exhibitions of the Lumiére Cinématographe, which threatened to preempt Edison's group in claiming ownership of the new invention.[26]

The Introduction of Projected Motion Pictures

It was agreed "that in order to secure the largest profit in the shortest time it is necessary that we attach Mr. Edison's name in some prominent capacity to this new [Armat] machine... We should not of course misrepresent the facts to any enquirer...."[27] Despite Edison's assurances to the contrary, by the time public exhibition was imminent, Armat had been rendered invisible and the invention was heralded as yet another triumph for the "Wizard of Menlo Park." For example, the *New York Dramatic Mirror,* March 5, 1986, announced that "the Vitascope, on which Thomas A. Edison has been working for years, and which he has at last perfected, will be exhibited at Koster & Bial's...." The projector used by ☐Edison on April 23, 1896, at Koster & Bial's Music Hall, an event that marks what is generally accepted as the first showing of motion pictures before a paying audience in the United States, the projector used by Edison was an adaptation of Armat's Phantascope. During the first week of the exhibition, Armat operated the projector.[28]

Koster & Bial's, located on Broadway at 34th Street where Macy's now stands, was one of the city's preeminent vaudeville houses. Many of the acts that had been photographed at the Black Maria as Kinetoscope subjects, such as Sandow the strong man and Carmencita, the dancer, had first been vaudeville attractions at Koster & Bial's. The theater's management had agreed to pay Raff & Gannon $800 per week for the attraction's four-month run. The eighth and final act of vaudeville that first evening, was "Thomas A. Edison's Latest Marvel, The Vitascope." Musser has determined that the Vitascope presentation consisted of six films. The first was a hand-tinted print of *Umbrella Dance*, with the Leigh Sisters. Next came *Rough Sea at Dover,* followed by *Walton and Slavin,* a comic boxing bout, then *Finale of 1st Act of Hoyt's "Milk White Flag,"* followed by *The Monroe Doctrine*, a flag-waver that in cartoon style showed Uncle Sam kicking John Bull out of Venezuela, a reference to a recent incident in South America. The program concluded with *Skirt Dance.*[29]

One reviewer assured his readers that "those who are familiar with the workings of the Kinetoscope will understand what the Vitascope is," except "that the pictures are thrown on a screen." He described the evening's program, commented on the audience's approval--despite unease in the front row as breaking waves approached--and concluded that "The Vitascope is a big success, and Mr. Edison is to be congratulated for his splendid contribution to the people's pleasure."[30]

Two months later, on June 29, another vaudeville house, Keith's Union Square Theater announced the

> First Exhibition in America of the Celebrated 'Lumiére's Cinématographe' The Sensation of Europe Exhibited before all the crowned heads and hailed universally as the Greatest marvel of the 19th Century....

in addition to a "big vaudeville show." Orchestra seats were fifty cents, and balcony seats twenty-five cents; typical of most first class vaudeville houses, these were prices only a moneyed or middle-class audience could then afford.[31]

The success of Lumiére's Cinématographe is affirmed by Grau, who states he was personally familiar with the management of the New Union Square, that he attended two shows a week at the theater, and that receipts went from $3500 to $7500 per week as a result of the moving-picture attraction.[32] Yet, as Grau points out, no craze for moving pictures developed, because, once the initial novelty wore off, the films were not extremely interesting. And so, within months of the medium's commercial introduction, announcements of program changes and "new" footage became significant, as seen in this excerpt from the *New York Times*

> Edison's Vitascope will be the main attraction at Proctor's Pleasure Palace this week. A number of new views have been arranged, including the arrival of Li Hung Chang, the firing of cannon at the Peekskill encampment, the sinking of the Rosedale, and the arrival of an elevated train at the Twenty-third Street Station.[33]

It should also be noticed that emphasis was shifting from filmed versions of vaudeville acts, to ones representing real events, which viewers and the trade began calling "actualities."

Another of Edison's competitors, American Mutoscope Company, now presented its projector, the Biograph, which made its New York theatrical debut on October 12, 1896, at the Olympia Music Hall. The Biograph was a "big hit," according to the *New York Times*. The film gauge used by the Biograph was twice as large as that used by the Vitascope, and the projected picture was considerably clearer and more lifelike. Further, the Biograph camera employed film-feeding mechanisms that were not dependent on previous patents. The film was transported by friction, rather than gears, and sprockets were punched into the film as it was exposed, so that American Mutoscope Company was able to apply for its own patents.[34]

The introduction of the Vitascope had opened the floodgates; within months competing systems were being used by exhibitors throughout the city. There was Edison's Vitascope at Koster & Bial's, as well as at Proctor's Pleasure Palace and Twenty-third Street Theater, Lumiére's Cinématographe at Keith's Union Square Theater, and American Mutoscope's Biograph at the Olympia Music Hall. Most observers agreed that of the three systems, the Vitascope had the least satisfactory picture. As the Biograph offered the sharpest, clearest, most realistic pictures, in short order many exhibitors had switched from Vitascope to other systems, primarily the Biograph. In fact, not long after the debut of the Vitascope, Edison dropped the Vitascope name and began marketing an improved model, the Projecting Kinetoscope, also known as the Projectoscope.[35]

Historian Robert C. Allen has pointed out that, because a well-established network of vaudeville theaters was conveniently in place throughout the nation when projected moving pictures were ready to be introduced, an "instant national audience" was accessible to the producers, without the need "to invest precious capital" in building theaters.[36] Once films were introduced, middle-class vaudeville theaters would continue as the primary venue for moving pictures until about 1906, when, as we will see, storefront theaters and nickelodeons began to predominate.

A few months after the Vitascope's introduction, America's vaudeville house patrons were talking about *The May Irwin Kiss*. May Irwin was a noted theatrical actress who had had a stage hit with *The Widow Jones*, in which the highlight was when she was kissed by actor John Rice. Eager for material, especially that which had the patina of the legitimate theater, for its middle-class, primarily male audience, Vitascope had bought the moving picture rights to this scene from Ms. Irwin, and released the film via the Orpheum chain of vaudeville theaters located in cities throughout the country. Laughable by today's standards, this sixty-second unctuous osculation, with the couple managing a side-of-the-mouth conversation during the act, was a sensation in 1896. As projector operators could repeat any scene instantly, audiences would demand six or seven encores of *The May Irwin Kiss*.[37]

Reactions of the First Middle-Class Audiences

It is reasonable to assume that of the people who filled Koster & Bial's on the evening of the Vitascope's introduction, a fair number were already familiar with the Kinetoscope, and therefore with the idea of pictures that moved. Many present were from the press or were merely curious vaudeville patrons. The venue, the formality of the occasion, and the price of admission ensured a predominantly middle-class audience. Terry Ramsaye recalled that "audiences were as full of silk hats as an undertaker's convention." The reviewer for the *New York Dramatic Mirror* reported that "the large audience testified its approval of the novelty by the heartfelt kind of applause." The audience's uncertainty in distinguishing illusion from reality in reaction to certain scenes was also noted:

> The second picture represented the breaking of waves on the seashore. Wave after wave came tumbling on the sand, and as they struck, broke into tiny floods just like the real thing. Some of the people in the front rows seemed to be afraid they were going to get wet, and looked about to see where they could run to, in case the waves came too close.[38]

Two months later, covering the introduction of the Cinématographe at Keith's Union Square at a "special morning matinee for the press," the *Dramatic Mirror* reported the images were "so life-like that the blasé scribes were moved to applaud," and that The Charge of the Seventh French Cuirassiers "was very inspiring." However, "The best picture was The Arrival of the Mail Train," in which

> the train came into the station, passengers alighted, met their friends and walked about, and all the bustle incident to affairs of this kindwas shown to perfection.[39]

A report a week later described "very enthusiastic" audiences who "wildly applauded" certain scenes, including the "stirring arrival of an express train."[40]

An "inspiring" cavalry charge? A "stirring" train arrival? Clearly, more than the depiction of these events was informing the audience's response. To some extent, the live orchestral accompaniment in these leading vaudeville houses helped establish the mood. Perhaps more important was the belief in moving pictures as the latest manifestation of a booming science that had recently brought forth the electric power and light that was now beginning to grace middle-class homes--a technology that could even make pictures come to life. It was as an appreciation of the miracles of science--its ability to reproduce motion within a real, actual setting and capture every detail of that motion--that audiences could outwardly demonstrate their feelings, which were often heightened when the subject matter was of a patriotic nature.

The respect for science and the sense of endless spectacle and detail absorbed by an entranced audience was captured by Henry Tyrell in July 1896, writing about moving-picture exhibitions in New York for *The Illustrated American*.

> The pictures shown are not only popular object-lessons in modern science, but they are charming in themselves, and for the images they evoke in the imagination. Sea-waves dash against a pier, or roll in and break languidly on the sandy beach, as in a dream; and the emotion produced upon the spectator is far more vivid than the real scene would be, because of the startling suddenness with which it is conjured up and changed, there in the theatre, by the magic wand of electricity. Street scenes, railway trains in motion, boxing-bouts, bull-fights and military evolutions are projected in life-like animation upon the luminous screen, while the audience sit spellbound in darkness. [41]

Perhaps the audience was too spellbound. An early producer, who also served as a projectionist, recalled that the second showing of the Black Diamond Express train (at Pastor's theater in New York) "almost ended in disaster," with the theater manager running into the projection booth and screaming, "Turn that goddamned thing off! Two ladies in the audience have fainted." [42] One "somewhat alarmed" man told the *New York Telegram* in 1896:

> When you can throw a picture of an express train on a screen in such a realistic way that persons who see it scramble to get out of its way and faint from fright, it's about time to stop... [43]

Comparisons between theatrical stage performances and moving pictures were almost immediate. In the *New York Herald*, in 1899, one writer, reviewing a stage performance of *Ben Hur,* noted

> In the play we see merely several horses galloping on a moving platform. They make no headway, and the moving scenery behind them does not delude the spectators into the belief that they are racing. The only way to secure the exact scene of action for this incident in a theater is to represent it by Mr. Edison's invention. [44]

Moving pictures were clearly changing audience expectations. Several live horses galloping on a theater stage had been reduced to a "merely."

The Alteration of Modes of Perception

Upton Sinclair remembered his first visits to the Eden Musee, a high-class waxworks that also featured moving pictures on New York's 23rd Street.

> ...you went into a little court, with palm and rubber trees, and sat in rows of chairs, and there was the image of the Twentieth Century Limited. It trembled and jumped so that it almost put your eyes out, but nevertheless it was so real that you could hardly keep from ducking out of the way as it bore down upon you. A tremendous adventure! [45]

Edward Wagenknecht stated that, "to even begin to understand how my contemporaries and I reacted to these early films," it was essential to accept "the now almost incomprehensible fact that what we were fascinated by primarily was mere movement itself." What moved or why was of little concern; "the important thing was movement itself." He pointed out that

> Nobody had ever seen a picture move before, and unless you keep that in mind you will be puzzled by our response to the Empire State Express rounding a curve or R. W. Paul's picures of surf breaking upon the shore at Dover.[46]

Because moving pictures were being exhibited in vaudeville houses, the exhibitors (and manufacturers) thought of them as one part of a regular vaudeville program. The typical vaudeville routine lasted fifteen or twenty minutes, so the film part of the program was expected to last that long. Since each film lasted only a minute or so, about a dozen films were required for each program.

At these early exhibitions, the delay between films was about twenty seconds, during which time the projectionist would change reels and thread the film.[47] Rather than considering this an intrusion, audiences apparently welcomed this respite as an opportunity to digest and discuss the film they had just seen. Because there was little narrative connection or continuity between films, no sense of interruption was produced. As late as 1912, manuals on the subject of moving picture exhibition recommended such breaks between films.[48]

Albert Smith, an early film pioneer and one of the founders of Vitagraph Studios, recalled that producers of the time did not consider that it might be possible to tell a story by film. "It was motion alone that intrigued the spectators; they exclaimed over clouds that floated, branches that waved, and smoke that puffed."[49] Curls of smoke were particularly enchanting for more than one reviewer, and fascination with the details of movement is evident in early descriptions of moving pictures. A Rochester, New York, writer described an exhibition of Lumiere's Cinematographe which would

> begin its fifteenth consecutive week at the Wonderland next week, continuing what was long ago the longest run made by any one attraction in this city. People go to see it again and again, for eventhe familiar views reveal some new feature with each successive exhibition. Take, for example, Baby's Breakfast, shown last week and this. It represents Pappa and Mamma fondly feeding the junior member of the household. So intent is the spectator usually in watching the proceedings of the happy trio at table that he fails to notice the pretty background of trees and shrubbery, whose waving branches indicate that a stiff breeze is blowing. So it is in each of the pictures shown;

they are full of interesting little details that come out one by one when the same views are seen several times....[50]

The reviewer's last two sentences reveal just some of the sense of wonder with which this medium was greeted; they also indicate that viewers were learning *how* to watch movies. Within a short time, among middle-class audiences, such phenomena would be absorbed in a glance and taken for granted. Later audiences, consisting largely of the working class, would have to educate themselves in similar fashion.

A reporter for the *New York Mail* noted that moving pictures of Major William McKinley, a presidential candidate, would be shown that night at Hammerstein's Olympia, and cautioned that the figures would "appear so perfectly natural that only the preinformed will know that they are looking upon shadow, not upon substance." The following day the *Mail* described the (largely Republican) audience reaction when McKinley appeared on screen "'in the flesh,' pandemonium broke loose for five minutes. Men stood up on their chairs and yelled with might and main..." To satisfy the audience, the film was repeated several times.[51]

The Popularity of Moving Pictures Weakens

It was unlikely that such an enraptured state could last. Toward the end of 1897, business began to soften. It was not that movies suddenly became unpopular, but that the sense of wonder had diminished. The novelty of seeing projected movement had begun to wear off, especially for those patrons who had actually come to see the vaudeville acts, and who were now getting bored with the brief, more or less plotless films.

By 1900, vaudeville houses were using the moving picture segments of their shows as "chasers," to clear the house after each show, on the premise that no one would want to sit through that part twice.[52] There has been some debate among film historians on this point. Allen contends that films were not actually used as chasers, as we refer to them, during this period, and cites contemporary sources to buttress his claim. Others, including Grau and Smith (who were contemporaries in the era), as well as Musser, North, Jowett, Mast and Jacobs, lend credence to the chaser theory. My own research has revealed that many contemporary claims stated outright or supported the notion that films were used as chasers, and I have favored that premise in this study.

Edison's film sales, which had reached $84,771 in 1987, dropped to $75,250 in 1898, $41,207 in 1899 and $38, 991 in 1900. Eastman Kodak, the major domestic supplier of film stock, saw its sales fall from $134,654 in 1899, to $104,425 in 1900, $85,317 in 1901, and not much better, $89,153 in 1902.[53]

The Spanish-American War, the imaginative films of George Melies, such as *A Trip to the Moon* (1902), or Edwin S. Porter's *The Great Train Robbery* (1903) created temporary stirs, but for the most part, in the vaudeville theaters of big cities, the motion-picture business was dormant.

Elsewhere, itinerant entrepreneurs were bringing to the hinterlands the wonders of moving pictures. A few months after the Vitascope's introduction, Raff & Gammon had offered projectors for rental on a "territorial rights" basis (a system that allowed the purchaser exclusive rights to a geographic area), and hopeful exhibitors had quickly exceeded the company's ability to deliver machines. While production and (because of population density) theaters were centered in the New York/New Jersey area, exhibitions also began to take place throughout the country. William T. Rock, a showman (and eventual partner in the formation of Vitagraph Studio), bought the Vitascope rights to Louisiana for $1,500 and, after a three-month run in New Orleans, moved on to smaller cities across the state, showing the same films in each.[54] Almost twenty years later Rock wrote, "We were the only state's rights owners out of about forty who made good with the Vitascope; all the others went broke on the deal."[55]

One possible explanation of why the others went broke is provided by an 1916 article in *Moving Picture World*, that suggests it was caused by ignorance and inexperience. Citing the career of Alfred E. Howard, an early distributor of Kinetoscope and Vitascope machines in New England, the article mentions that

> His customers came principally from shoe workers, grocers, textile hands, and others from the mill towns, who, hearing of the new moving pictures, came to Boston, bought an outfit with a couple of films, and started in the show business. Ninety percent of these ventures were failures, principally from the fact that the men had no knowledge of electricity, knew nothing of the moving picture machine, were in total ignorance of the show business....[56]

Other showmen toured the country, offering moving-picture exhibitions in towns far removed from population centers. In New England, for example, traveling exhibitors took advantage of local customs, utilizing legitimate theaters in which to present "educational lectures" on Sundays (when they were ordinarily closed) and played to capacity audiences. Their success provided theater owners a glimpse of the medium's commercial potential.[57] Lyman E. Howe, perhaps the most persistent of the traveling exhibitors, used a projector called the Animatiscope, and toured

24

small cities and towns with great success, although his prices were not cheap. In Ithaca, New York, Howe's presentation to the Ladies' Alliance of the Unitarian Church was so well attended that a second engagement a month later drew a capacity crowd of 850 who paid twenty-five cents apiece. Howe's program was varied, consisting of "songs, conversations, etc., well given by the phonograph, after which pictures of moving picture objects were thrown upon the screen."[58]

Ithaca had a number of moving-picture exhibitions in 1897. For example, Howe presented his show on May 8 and June 9; the Renwick Beach Amusement Park presented a Vitascope reenactment of the Corbett-Fitzsimmons fight in August, although the projection was inadequate and patrons' money had to be refunded. On October 4 and 5 the Lyceum Theater offered moving pictures of the real Corbett-Fitzsimmons fight, using a Veriscope projector and charging seventy-five, fifty, or twenty-five cents; also in October, Library Hall presented three successive nights of variety programing, which included moving pictures shown with a Biograph projector; and on December 10, The Lyceum offered a variety program with films shown by an Animatograph projector. While Ithaca was a college town and, as North reminds us, not altogether typical, practically every town whose population could support a twenty-five-cent (and up) moving-picture exhibition soon found itself visited by itinerant showmen.[59]

One reason for moving from town to town was the lack of fresh films, which were usually available from only one supplier, the Edison Company, although competitive projector manufacturers like American Mutoscope produced their own films for customers. In those days, manufacturers would provide projector, projectionist and films for each presentation in big-city vaudeville houses. While those theaters could rely on live acts to fill their hour-long programs, traveling exhibitors had to rely almost exclusively on projected images.

Magic lantern slides were used extensively as "filler," their steady image often providing welcome relief from the flickering moving pictures. The slides enabled exhibitors to offer a variety of subjects, similar in nature to the motion-picture part of the program. Advertisements in early trade journals display the types of slides available: "'The Tower of London,' twenty-four slides, 'A Day At the Zoo,' thirty slides, 'London,' fifty slides."[60] Despite this attempt at variety, using the limited number of films in their possession, once the occupants of a town had viewed the entire program, it was time for exhibitors to move on, showing the same films and slides in the next town.

Managers of traveling circuses and street carnivals took note of this new competition and adapted it for their use, setting up "black tents" in which moving pictures were shown, as part of their shows.[61] Exhibitors, whether itinerant or not, had a wide range of systems from which to choose. The Vitascope, Cinematographe and Biograph projecting machines were just the tip of the iceberg. In 1897, the *Literary Digest* provided a "comprehensive list" of moving picture projecting systems, a virtual cornucopia of "scopes" and "graphs." Among the 52 designations listed were such curiosities as the Chronophotographoscope, the Craboscope, the Katoptikum and the Lobsterscope.[62]

At this point the dominant venues for moving pictures were vaudeville theaters in cities, and traveling shows in rural areas. The field was being developed by men with a bent for machines--inventors and hobbyists who were fascinated with the mechanics of projection, but not particularly mindful of its aesthetic potential. Not just the general public, but most of the press, as well as politicians, civic leaders and educators, accepted this technological view of the medium. These men, who envisioned industries built primarily around the manufacturing and selling of moving-picture machines, controlled the industry for most of its first decade.

More than seven years after their introduction, moving pictures were still simply one of the acts in a vaudeville program. Jowett has stated that "their exploitation by the vaudeville houses was the 'lowest point' in motion picture history, and almost succeeded in killing off the new medium."[63]

2. THE WORKING CLASS: THE NEGLECTED MARKET

Immigration: the Second Wave

Although moving-pictures were languishing among the initial middle-class audiences, new venues were being explored in the working-class areas of major cities. For while the urban middle class was being wildly astonished and then eventually bored by moving pictures, working-class people were barely conscious of the new medium's existence. Because of the cost of admittance, as well as the inaccessibility of vaudeville theaters (which were usually located in middle-class entertainment centers), the working class had been largely excluded from participation in this new form of entertainment.

My claim is that the immigrant population itself constituted the market that enabled motion-picture manufacturers to survive and restructure their business to accommodate a larger, more economically diverse audience. But what was it that made this impoverished, powerless population so critical at this juncture? Why did the immigrant working class embrace movies just as the middle class was rejecting them? First, however, we must know who these people were and the circumstances of their living conditions.

The factor that most influences the destinies of immigrants to the United States as a group is the year of their entry. Immigration for the period under study here is usually differentiated by chronology. The first wave, or "old immigration," began in about 1830, bringing in vast numbers of Western Europeans--Germans, Scandinavians and Irish; while the second wave, or "new immigration," which began about 1880, consisted primarily of Eastern Europeans--Russians, Italians, Poles and Slavs.

Most immigrants came to America in search of what the Jews called the "Goldeneh Medina", or the Golden Land. What they usually found was a life of

27

toil, with little hope of permanent economic betterment. The rurally based new immigrants, Slavs, Jews and Italians, who poured into the United States discovered a nation far different from that encountered by their old-immigrant predecessors. The Germans and Scandinavians of the first wave had dispersed throughout the country, many finding success as farmers or merchants. Several of the German Jews of the first wave, like Strauss and Gimbel, had begun as common street peddlers and become founders of great fortunes. Their names were synonymous with the growth taking place in America.[1]

The earlier, old immigrants had been needed to settle the virgin lands of the western territories and to build the railroads required by an expanding nation. Free land, given by the government to anyone willing to work it, was still available. But by 1882 when the new immigrants began to arrive, the frontier was gone, and the need for labor was in the rapidly growing industrial sectors. The new immigrants, usually arriving penniless, had little choice other than employment in the sweatshops and factories located in or near urban centers.[2]

While the image of the poor Eastern European immigrant arriving in the United States, living in an overcrowded ghetto, finding employment and slowly rising into the lower middle class, may be a reassuring one--and did on occasion actually happen--it was not true for the vast majority of immigrants, who worked hard all their lives and saw little, if any, improvement in their economic fortunes. Nor is it wholly true that immigrants were already accustomed to the deprivation they experienced in the United states. Among them, it was the relatively literate who tended to emigrate to other countries. As Bodnar has shown, the greater the illiteracy, the shorter was the distance moved.[3]

By the time the second wave arrived, the immigrants of the first wave had already negotiated an alien environment and for the most part had opted to leave the cities. But those who remained managed to arrange specific social relationships by selecting living quarters according to the degree of their familiarity with the culture around them. Where possible they tended to settle in neighborhoods whose populations were similar to themselves, and where the language and customs could be understood. The new immigrants followed this same pattern, which meant following in the footsteps of those who had arrived before them.[4] Sometimes the influx was so great that the host city adapted the character of the newly dominant population--Poles in Pittsburgh, Irish in Boston, Irish and Scandinavian in Worcester.

The influx from Europe became considerable in size. In 1870, only 3,000 Italians and a handful of Jews entered the United States. In the 1880s, 270,000 Italians and 160,000 Jews were admitted, and in the 1890s an additional 600,000 Italians and 344,000 Jews had immigrated to the United States. Between 1900 and 1910, two million Italians and one million Jews entered the country; this was before World War I drastically reduced the flow.[5] New York, as the nation's primary immigration entry point, was host to a patchwork of ethnic neighborhoods that accommodated members of both old and new immigrations. In 1906, a study in Italy of destinations mentioned in passport application records indicated that New York City was the destination of 30 percent of the applicants, with Chicago named by 17 percent and Pittsburgh, 10 percent. Cleveland was a distant fourth at 4 percent.[6]

With little money, many could go no further than their city of entry. In the years 1900 to 1910, for example, Italians brought an average of $19.95 each with them, while Jews each had $29.09 to get them through their introduction to the New World. During that decade, one-third of the 10 million immigrants to pass through the city settled in New York, among them 700,000 Jews and one million Italians. Of other groups, one million Poles, and the majority of Hungarians, Croations and Slovenes had found their way to the factories, mines and mills of Pennsylvania.[7]

Between 1870 and 1915, New York City's population increased by more than 300 percent, from 1.5 to 5 million. This would be repeated under slightly similar circumstances fifty years later: As impoverished working-class ethnic groups moved to the inner city, the middle class moved out. Population figures confirm this. In 1870 more than 60 percent of the population of greater New York lived in Manhattan. By 1915, a little more than 40 percent resided there. While Manhattan's population more than doubled, the suburban or middle-class populations in Brooklyn, the Bronx and Queens multiplied by four, sixteen and nine respectively.[8] Such prejudices affected many aspects of city life that depended on middle-class participation. A Columbia University Dean decried the common opinion that the school's presence "at the gateway of European immigration" made it "socially uninviting to students who come from homes of refinement." He pointed out that the typical inquiry involved Columbia being "overrun with European Jews who are most unpleasant persons socially...."[9] This tendency by the middle class, whenever possible, to avoid associating with the working class, as I shall claim, was signified by the behavior of movie audiences in a way that provided a brief period of autonomy for the working class audience.

By 1900, the foreign-born and their children constituted over 76 percent of New York City's population, so that the city was, to an increasing extent, a patchwork of neighborhoods representing myriad ethnic and religious groups. Jacob Riis observed that the one thing you could not find "in the chief city of America is a distinctively American community. There is none; certainly not among the tenements."[10] Contemporary reports document the living conditions in the slums occupied by the working poor in the major urban centers. Regardless of the particular city, the conditions are consistently cited for their endangerment to health and soul.

The Lower East Side

The Lower East Side of New York City is perhaps most renowned for, and most typical of, ghetto social and economic life. "I should feel as if I were exaggerating if I recorded my first impression of their loathsomeness," wrote William Dean Howells in 1896, referring to the living conditions in the area. A survey of 1908 showed that about half the families on the Lower East Side slept three or four to a room, and more than a third slept five or more to a room.[11]

Although Emma Lazarus had characterized them as "wretched refuse," in her famous sonnet, historian Loren Baritz has emphasized that

> For all the afflictions the immigrants suffered, it is not likely that many felt like wretched refuse. What they did feel like was poor--not the same thing, except to Americans, who equate culture with money.

Nor did the residents of the Lower East Side harbor any sentimental illusions about the area: as soon as it was economically possible, they moved out. In the early 1890s, three-quarters of all Jews in New York lived on the Lower East Side. By 1903, this figure had dropped to 50 percent.[12]

In 1890, the density of population per acre in New York City as a whole was about sixty people, and about 115 people per acre in Manhattan, But on the Lower East Side, in the Tenth Ward (a Jewish area that included Orchard and Hester streets), the population density was 522 people per acre. According to Riis, the area was the most densely populated on earth, "China not excluded." Nor did matters improve. By 1900 the figure would reach 700 people per acre. Cleanliness, among other things, was a problem. When social workers Lillian Wald and Mary Brewster moved to the Lower East Side, they sought one of the two bathrooms said to exist in the tenements below 14th Street. When they finally located one, it was in the hall.[13]

Yet this was not necessarily the viewpoint of the immigrant: Mary Antin, imagining how condescendingly a typical middle-class sightseer would have described her family's first dingy tenement apartment in America, wrote:

> But I saw a very different picture on my introduction to Union Place [in Boston]. I saw two imposing rows of brick buildings, loftier than any dwelling I had ever lived in. Brick was even on the ground for me to tred on, instead of common earth or boards.[14]

The streets of the Lower East Side reflected the cultural diversity of the area and revealed to the knowing eye its particular uniqueness. For example, the sale of men's clothing dominated both Hester and Stanton streets. But the garments of Hester Street were for the most part second-hand, while Stanton's were new. Cherry Street, surrounded by Jewish tenements, was at one point completely Irish and Catholic.[15]

The work day (when there was work) was long, and pay was inadequate. One resident recalled that, despite six working family members (his father and five siblings), "their aggregate earnings provided the barest subsistence for us."[16] In most working class homes, all members of the family who could work, with the possible exception of the mother, did so. Though often a wage-earner, a mother's time was also spent endlessly caring for the family--washing and ironing clothes, shopping and cooking, sewing, and in some cases making the clothes the family wore.[17]

This was a status not always willingly accepted. Writing of Jewish women, Hutchins Hapgood noticed that

> The passionate feeling at the bottom of most of their 'tendency' beliefs is that woman should stand on the same social basis as man, and should be weighed on the same scales. This ruling creed is held by all classes of the educated women of the ghetto....[18]

The experiences of the Baline family, arriving penniless in New York in 1893, are somewhat typical. Moses Baline, the father, had been a rabbi in Russia, but in America the best he could do was become a poultry inspector, which paid so poorly he resorted to house painting to earn money. His wife Lena became a midwife. Their three daughters (a fourth had died young) "found occasional employment wrapping cigars, another common trade for immigrant women...the oldest of the boys...toiled in a sweatshop." The youngest son, Izzy, age six or seven,

> worked as well, hawking the...*Evening Journal* on the street....
> Every evening when he and the rest of the Baline children came

home from work, they would deposit the coins they had earned...
into Lena's outspread apron. [19]

Budget studies during this period for the nation as a whole indicate that the average working-class family of four to six earned $800 a year, or $15 per week. However, social workers in new York City reported:

> The average wage for husbands whose wives were homemakers was under $500 a year....The average weekly income from the men's work was $3.81. The average monthly was $10. The average family size was four and a half.

The report pointed out that because one month's rent took more than two week's wages, it was "evident that women must work or the family goes hungry."[20] "Homework," usually piecework that was brought home and performed by the whole family, was the common form of exploitation. Social workers found that

> over 13,000 New York tenement houses were licensed by the Bureau of Factory Inspection of the State Department of Labor as places where work given out by manufacturers and contractors could be made or finished, "where the labor of all members of the family can be utilized without reference to age or factory law."[21]

A sixty-hour week was the average for shop workers. Homework usually required eighty-four hours a week for the laborer. With money so dear and hard-earned, working-class leisure activities had to be extremely inexpensive. The most common recreational activities were free. As often as not, leisure consisted of sitting in front of the house, or visiting nearby relatives. An excursion to a place like Coney Island was a treat for rarely more than a once or twice a year. Peiss has noted that the streets "served as the center of social life," with people gathering on street corners, stoops and in doorways to socialize.[22]

Michael Davis, in a study for the Russell Sage Foundation of New York's working class in 1911, pointed out that in earlier days a home meant a house big enough for a large family

> to sleep and eat, work and play in. All the natural activities of life centered themselves about the home....The city changes all this. The home shrinks to a nest of boxes tucked four stories in the air, or the half of a duplex house huddled upon its neighbors. There is space to sleep and eat, but none to live. The habitation becomes a sleeping box and eating den--too often, no more. [23]

The ingrained cruelty of ghetto life could also be revealed. Chotzinoff recalled his first day on Stanton Street, watching from his tenement window as some boys with their pocket knives skinned a dead, fly-covered horse lying in the gutter.[24]

For James Huneker, looking back, all this was enchantingly "picturesque," an area in which "magazine writers had not topsy-turvied the ideas of the tenement dwellers, nor were the street-cleaner, the Board of Health, and other destroyers of the picturesque in evidence."[25]

Immigrant workers in the areas outside the crowded cities fared little better--and often worse--than their metropolitan counterparts. In 1910, the mill town of Homestead, Pennsylvania, a suburb of Pittsburgh, was studied by Margaret Byington for the Russell Sage Foundation. Similarities between the social conditions and economic fortunes of the inhabitants seem clear.

Homestead had a population of about 13,000, "chiefly mill workers and their families," whose primary employment was in the Carnegie steel mills of the United States Steel Corporation, which dominated the town. The population was equally divided between second-generation native whites, native-born whites of foreign parents, and foreign-born whites. In the mills themselves, about 28 percent of the employees (and most of the management) were native whites, while 70 percent were immigrant stock. More than half of all employees were Slavs, recently arrived in the second wave. Similarly to what occurred on the Lower East Side, as the new immigrants moved in, the previous immigrants, primarily English and German, moved out. Byington noted that,

> As German and British tend to amalgamate with the native whites the community has fallen more or less naturally into two major groups-- the English-speaking and the Slavs.[26]

A mill employee's day shift began at 7:00 a.m. and ended at 5:50 p.m., six days a week; there was an equivalent night shift. More than 72 percent of the Slavic workers earned less than $12 per week, while fewer than 8 percent of the English-speaking British, Irish or German employees earned that little.[27] In all, the Carnegie Pittsburgh plants employed more than 14,000 common laborers, nearly 12,000 of them from South and Eastern Europe. There was little regard for workers' safety in these mills; between 1907 and 1910, in each year, nearly 25 percent of immigrant employees were killed or injured on the job.[28]

Water from the town was drawn from the Monongahela River, contaminated by runoff from industrial cities upstream as well as by chemically impregnated drainage from local mines. As one resident put it, "No respectable microbe would live in it."

A study of the death rate in 1907 (24 per 1000) showed that 38.2 percent of these deaths were "...from diseases closely connected with lack of sufficient air, good food, and intelligent care of children."[29]

Leisure and Working-Class Men and Women

In the cities with large working-class populations such as New York, men could extend the boundaries of their leisure pursuits with visits to the saloon, lodge or club. Lodges and clubs were usually fraternal or mutual-benefit organizations that were started by working people. Others were sponsored by a church, like the Workingman's Club of the Church of the Holy Communion. Unterstutsung Vereinen (health societies) were formed by German immigrants, usually based on their occupation or place of birth. There were over 2,000 Italian societies, each composed of immigrants from a particular town or vicinity. One such benevolent order, the Societa di Mutuo-Soccorso Isola Salina (Salina Island Society of Loans-Assistance), limited membership to those born on Salina. Jews had been the first to organize mutual benefit societies. Russian Jewish men tended to spend much of their leisure time at public lectures, libraries or in night school. Hungarians and Czechs had their own clubs and workmen circles. Club membership was not always separated from the saloon. Of 702 such clubs surveyed, almost 70 percent met in saloons or establishments that sold liquor.[30]

In Homestead, athletic clubs established by the community, ostensibly for the working class, tended to be the province of clerical and professional workers rather than mill workers. The latter were "too tired after their hours of heavy work." There were, however, more than 50 saloons in the town and, "as places of relaxation, they fill a need not therefore supplied."[31]

While workmen could attend saloons, clubs, lodges, pool rooms and union meetings, working-class women were shut out of what Peiss terms the homosocial world of leisure. These women had little time for recreation. Their work began before the men woke up, so that breakfast would be ready, and ended long after the men had finished their day's labor. The leisure time for women often blended in with their work, such as "going shopping" with a friend, or sewing circles in which women could simultaneously work and socialize. One disapproving tenement inspector noted that many women tended to do their laundry in the yard. "Besides being the playground of children, it is the gathering vestibule for gossip and exchange for profanity."[32]

34

For single working women, however, the fact of employment meant a certain degree of independence and exposure to other forms of recreation. In 1900, four-fifths of all wage-earning women were single, and one-third were between sixteen and twenty years old. In New York, where many department stores, sweatshops, factories and offices provided an expanding job market, nearly 60 percent of all women in the sixteen- to twenty-year age group worked. The most popular forms of entertainment for these women were "cheap theater," a form of vaudeville that played in local theaters at reduced prices (ten, fifteen and twenty cents, as opposed to the twenty-five, thirty-five and fifty cents charged by standard vaudeville houses) and dance halls. Of the two, dancing was by far the more popular with working-class women. One social worker counted thirty-one dance halls on the Lower East Side, a greater concentration than in any other section of the city.[33]

According to at least one writer, the reason for the popularity of dancing was simple:

> Dancing is the one real amusement within the working girl's means....for five cents the cheaper 'dancing academies' of the East Side give a whole evening's pleasure. For the domestic servant and poorer shopping girl of the East Side there is practically no option, if she is to have any enjoyment of her youth....[34]

But even the relatively low cost of both entertainments was too expensive to allow the women frequent attendance, which to a large degree depended on being "treated" by men, with the expectation of sexual favors this often implied. Immigrant parents were opposed to the dance halls, not without cause. Dance halls, according to Elizabeth Ewen, "embodied the seamy side of urban culture. The instructors were often pimps and procurers."[35]

Typical of many female factory workers, Yeddie Bruker earned seven dollars per week, and spent four dollars on room and board. Two dollars were spent on clothes, and sixteen cents on union dues. Her recreation budget was ten cents, which she usually spent on theater tickets.[36]

For working class families in other areas of the country, the choices allowed little improvement. In Homestead during good times, out of a weekly expenditure of $18.79 (which signified the relatively high wages of a male, rather than a female factory worker), a typical family spent sixty-seven cents on recreation. During hard times, with only half-time work available, out of a total weekly expenditure of $10.63, eleven cents was spent on recreation.[37]

In describing the deprivations of her Boston slum home, Mary Antin sensed the necessity for a public space that would fulfill, even fleetingly, the social needs of ghetto-bound families.

> Beds and cribs took up most of the floor space, disorder packed theinterspaces. The centre table in the 'parlor' was not loaded with books. It held, invariably, a photograph album and an ornamental lamp with a paper shade; and the lamp was usually out of order. So there was as little motive for a common life as there was room. The yard was only big enough for the perennial rubbish heap. The narrow sidewalk was crowded. What were the people to do with themselves?[38]

3. THE ERA OF PARTICIPATION (1905-1912)

Development of Working-Class Venues

In 1905, vaudeville was still the preferred initial outlet for a new moving picture. The location and relative luxury of the vaudeville theater, as compared to the few small storefront theaters that were beginning to appear, provided a patina of quality and freshness to a film that was similar in nature to the later practice of opening a film in a prestigious first-run "downtown" theater before releasing it to second- and third-run neighborhood houses. The manufacturers charged more for brand new films, and vaudeville houses were better able to pay the price. A film like *The Great Train Robbery,* released in 1903, had been shown on practically every vaudeville circuit in the country. Two years later it was still being sold, though at reduced prices, among the black-tent shows in the hinterland, and "...the little five-cent store shows in the humbler tenderloins of our big cities."[1]

For historian Douglas Gomery, the years between 1902 and 1905 were a "vacuum," during which "Motion pictures had no permanent home." In vaudeville theaters, the moving picture was just one of many acts--and not a particularly successful act at that; in all other venues, such as traveling shows and carnivals, they were offered in an unpredictable, itinerant mode of distribution.[2] But in large cities all over the country, most significantly in New York, entrepreneurs were taking the tentative steps that would uncover the market of "undesirables" whose pennies and nickels would provide the capital for expansion and enable forays appealing to the highly coveted middle-class market. No one knows when the first storefront theater opened; certainly, because of the conditions of their social existence, immigrants represented a waiting market.

In Pittsburgh, in June 1905, Harry Davis, the city's most prominent and wealthy vaudeville entrepreneur, opened a small, 96-seat theater exclusively for the purpose of showing moving pictures and without the benefit of any live acts. Davis called his theater "The Nickelodeon." Although it was not the first theater to show films exclusively (there had been several storefront theaters before this), the name caught on. Movie theaters were sometimes referred to as "nickelettes" and other such names, but similar theaters became generically known as nickelodeons. Davis's theater, using props and decorations gleaned from his other theaters, had its name spread across the front entrance in thick, bulb-illuminated letters, and a ticket booth was placed in front of what would later be called an "outer lobby." These bits of not inexpensive glitz helped to differentiate nickelodeons from the storefront theaters requiring a lower investment. The Nickelodeon was soon grossing $1000 per week. Within a year, Davis had opened over eight more nickelodeons in Pittsburgh, and was starting to expand his operations to Buffalo, Philadelphia and Detroit.[3]

I would suggest that between the period of the vaudeville-house venue and the rise of the nickelodeon (most likely during 1903-1906) there was an interim stage consisting of what could be called "urban traveling shows" run by individuals who had managed--by rental or purchase--to acquire a projector and some films. They went from neighborhood to neighborhood, renting space for short periods of time and exhibiting films for as long as it took the people in the immediate vicinity to get bored with the presentation.

Admittedly, documenting this phenomenon is difficult, if not impossible, for several reasons. During this period, exhibitors could buy films and projectors outright, and could sell or trade their prints at will, so there are few known records of where these films were being shown. Further, these theaters did no advertising, relying on barkers to attract passing patrons, and by word of mouth. Although there is no documentation to support this contention, let me point out the ideal conditions for such activity.

For one thing, opening a storefront (or, as I would suggest, an apartment) theater was relatively inexpensive. Within a few years, once nickelodeons had been established, setting up a theater would require a substantial investment of several thousand dollars. But in the beginning, working-class audiences had minimum expectations regarding the quality of their theater's spatial surroundings, a factor that made such investments possible for low-capital entrepreneurs. In 1904, the Lubin Company advertised a complete moving picture set-up for a low bargain price:

> *Bold Bank Robbery*
> Length 600 ft. $60
> Cineograph/Stereopticon

```
        (projector)          75
    Two Cineograph films
        (100 ft. each)       22
    Two Monarch records for
        playing music with
        the films ($1 each)   2
                            $99  Total
```
<u>Plus</u> with each $99 order, a Victor Talking Machine
for playing records ($37.50 value).[4]

The fact that recorded music is assured implies that the potential purchaser was seen as one who would be on the move, necessarily sans piano.

Further, many projectors were portable and required no electricity, an important feature at a time when most tenement buildings lacked this new convenience; Lumiere's Cinematographe, for example, was hand-cranked and used limelight for illumination.[5] The practicality of short-term exhibition in working-class neighborhoods is suggested by William Fox who, in 1904, to save a failing penny arcade he owned, converted a second-floor apartment above it to a moving-picture theater, thereby discovering what a biographer called "a real gold mine."[6]

Miriam Cooper, who grew up in New York, had featured roles in *The Birth of A Nation* (1915) and *Intolerance* (1916). She remembered the cheap surroundings of the one movie show she saw (about 1904-1908) before actually appearing in some.

> The movie theater was just a vacant store. That's what most of them were back in those days.... Somebody would rent a store cheap and paint the windows black, both to make it dark and to keep people from looking in. For a nickel you could sit on folding chairs and watch figures in stark black and white move jerkily and silently on a dirty bed sheet.[7]

In Chicago, as Wagenknecht recalled the era, the theaters were similarly transitory in appearance, although offering a variation on painted windows.

> Many of the neighborhood theaters were merely converted stores. Sometimes they did not even trouble to remove the plate glass windows (after all, the building might be used for another purpose six months hence) but merely pasted the posters up against them on the inside....[8]

Immigrants and the Rapid Growth of Nickelodeons

Within a few years, these forays into working class neighborhoods had turned into an avalanche, or "explosion," according to many contemporary accounts. In 1906, *The Billboard* called nickelodeons the "jackrabbits" of the entertainment industry because "they multiply so rapidly." Another trade publication claimed they were multiplying faster than guinea pigs, and estimated there were 2,500 to 3,000 five-cent theaters in the United States. *Harper's Weekly* called it "nickel madness."[9]

In 1907, *Moving Picture World* commented on the sudden growth of nickelodeons and noted the amount in footage of "new film subjects" that had been released during previous months in response to demand,

1906	Feet
November.....	10,000
December......	11,000
1907	
January.........	12,000
February.......	14,000
March...........	28,000[10]

Joseph Medill Patterson, in the *Saturday Evening Post,* reported that "this line is a Klondike." He noted that

> three years ago there was not a nickelodeon...in America. Today there are between four and five thousand running and solvent.... This is the boom time in the moving-picture business. Everybody is making money--manufacturers, renters, jobbers, exhibitors.[11]

The nature of the audience was also of interest to Patterson. "In cosmopolitan city districts," he wrote, "the foreigners attend in larger proportion than the English speakers."[12]

It was not only in "cosmopolitan city districts" that a shift in audience was occurring. Contemporary reports and articles continuously remind the researcher that, in every part of the country, whether mill towns in New England or cities like Chicago or Pittsburgh, local writers were commenting on the largely working-class composition of nickelodeon audiences. The survey conducted by Davis in 1911 for the Russell Sage Foundation concluded that 72 percent of the moving-picture audience were working class. Czitrom states that a study of 1000 working-class men in 1914 indicated that "those working the longest hours spent the most time" in the nickelodeons, and "those who earned less than ten dollars per week went the most often."[13]

In 1910, a trade-paper reporter visited the moving-picture theaters in the Chicago ghetto, "that is, along Halsted Street, between 12th and 14th streets." He noted "There are several little theaters in this district, some of which offer vaudeville in Jewish, and some others which only show pictures." The reporter visited six "Jewish" theaters along Halsted, and mentioned that two blocks north there is a little theater patronized exclusively byItalians. The vaudeville consisted of a song and comic sketch in Italian, which brought a good many laughs.... North of this theater the population seems to be wholly Greek...the Palace theater at 18th and Halsted streets is another which depends on foreign people for its support. The people in this locality are mostly Polish or Slavish.[14]

The polyglot composition of the audience and its desire to experience the once-familiar pastoral environment so divorced from ghetto living, was recognized by one writer who observed that stories of

a Watteau shepherdess, posed, perhaps, in a modern wood just outside Paris, where real sheep are available, are quite real to the audience of a New York East Side nickelodeon, whether they are mentally interpreted in Yiddish, Italian, Bohemian, Syrian or Polish.[15]

In 1909, a researcher who had studied working women in Pittsburgh during 1907 and 1908, made special note of the throngs of women "packed thick...hot and tired and irritable," but waiting patiently in line at the Saturday five-cent show: "It was an incident not without significance, this eagerness with which they turned toward leisure after a working week of unmeaning hours...."[16] The coveted middle-class audience was developing very slowly. The working-class immigrant audience, however, was growing very quickly, making possible the "sudden explosion" in nickelodeons. Like most observers at the time, Patterson saw moving pictures as being of great benefit to the working class, but did not acknowledge that the working class was of even greater benefit to the industry.

While big-city vaudeville houses retained the middle class audience that was still interested in moving pictures, nickelodeons were opening wherever sufficient numbers of the working class settled. In 1907, a writer for *Moving Picture World* reported on movie business in Ohio; Muncie, had eight moving-picture theaters, and Youngstown had fifteen. Dayton had fourteen moving-picture theaters, and "everyone is crowded." Little Urbana, with a population of 6,000, had four theaters.[17] Another writer noted that Butler, New Jersey, "a small manufacturing town in the Ramapo Mountains," which with its neighboring town, Mooningdale, had a combined population of 4,000 to 5,000, "75% of whom are employed in the two mills in Butler," had at least one nickelodeon.[18]

An editorial in *The Willimantic Journal* described what was happening in that Connecticut town.

In a factory village like Willimantic there are hundreds of people whose only home here is the little sometime cold and cheerless room where they sleep...and before the advent of the five cent show they looked in vain for any other place [than saloons] more congenial....The men who formerly were rarely seen on the streets in company with their wives and children have come to the practice of taking their family for an hour almost nightly to the five-cent shows.[19]

Kingston, New York, with a population of 20,000, had four moving-picture theaters. Edward Armitage, at the time a middle-class youngster in Albany, New York, remembered he had to go to a working-class neighborhood to see a movie because that's where the theater was. Roanoke, Virginia, with a population of 30,000, had six moving-picture theaters, and only one of those featured vaudeville acts.[20] As a sign of the times, near the end of 1907, Koster & Bial's announced that henceforth moving pictures, along with song-slide presentations, would be the basis for future shows. Admittance would be five cents and ten cents. No seats would be reserved. And the name of the theater would be changed to the Bijou Dream.[21]

A little more than a year later, a *New York Times* headline noted "The Nation Wide Wave of Motion Pictures" and, in a sub-head, "How It Has Swept Over The Country Until It Represents An Investment of 40 Millions of Dollars and the Employment of 100,000 Persons."[22]

As we've seen, converting a store into a theater in an immigrant neighborhood was not a capital-intensive operation. In the working class neighborhoods, niceties were not required, and a theater could be set up with an initial investment of a few hundred dollars. Adolph Zukor, one of the founders of Paramount, recalled that

In those days you could buy a projection machine for $75 or $95. People with money or with a substantial business would never think of opening a little store show, but as long as it did not take more than $300 or $400 to open up a theater, a good many small investors took a chance....[23]

Nickelodeons' Location and their Audiences' Composition

No one really knows exactly how many neighborhood storefront (or apartment) theaters existed in New York City during this period. But the number must have been substantial and growing, for in 1908, as a result of a court decision, the Tenement House Department decided that henceforth no new moving-picture shows would be allowed in tenement houses.[24]

Robert C. Allen, citing *Trow's Business Directory* of 1908 and other sources, listed 123 places of moving-picture exhibition, exclusive of vaudeville houses, in Manhattan. Inasmuch as 1908 was a year of continuing rapid growth in the number of nickelodeons in New York and throughout the country, this figure can be

42

considered conservative. (In that same, year *Moving Picture World* estimated that there were 300 to 400 moving-picture theaters in the city.) Ben Singer stated that, when compared with a New York Police Commissioner's report on movie theaters, *Trow's* 1908 listed only about two-fifths of the theaters operating that year.

Forty-two of the theaters listed by Trow's, or about a third, were located on the Lower East Side. Of these, thirteen were on the Bowery, the city's major entertainment district. But twenty-nine were located on residential streets among the tenements. There were ten more nickelodeons in Jewish Harlem, an area between 98th and 118th streets and a northeast segment of Central Park to Lexington Avenue, extending to Park Avenue. The area was occupied by a mixture of first- and second-generation American Jews who had become successful enough to escape from the Lower East Side.

The Yorkville section, a German-Irish neighborhood bounded by 74th and 89th streets, Third Avenue and the East River, had nine movie theaters.[25] According to Laidlaw, "Little Italy" was bounded by 100th and 120th streets, and First and Third avenues, and thirteen movie theaters were packed into this relatively small area. The Italians who lived there, like the neighboring Jews of Jewish Harlem, had been able to escape the abject poverty of downtown ghettos. The total population of Little Italy was 27,406, of which 21,262 were Italian.[26] Although it has been claimed otherwise, in regard to the area between East 104th and 109th streets, evidence does not suggest it was a middle class neighborhood. A visiting researcher, E. Idell Zeisloft, commented in 1899 that "the tenements that line these streets are not much to look at," but "the gay lines of wash, the small shops and street scenes make up a picture that never loses interest" and that "the stiletto is rarely brought into play." However, Zeisloft described First Avenue as "from start to finish...an avenue of the poor." His appraisal of the general area was gloomy. "From the East River to Fifth Avenue on all of these streets [89th to 103rd] are tenements of the poorest class." He noted that, despite the "hint of an Italian settlement," Little Italy actually started several blocks to the north and, in that area, "some old houses, once private residences, remain: but for the most part the cheap new tenement is the fashion."[27]

Grace Mayer listed the occupations of the inhabitants as "fruit and vegetable and ice vending, dressmaking and tailoring, stone cutting, bootblacking, manufacturing macaroni...knife sharpening, organ grinding," all of which are clearly working-class occupations.[28] Given what we know about the relationship between income and movie attendance, the fact that a great many nickelodeons serviced this area would be a strong indication that it was a working-class, low- income neighborhood

If we accept this interpretation, we see that, out of 123 theaters, 74, or 60 percent, were located in immigrant and/or working-class neighborhoods. The remaining theaters were clustered in various areas around the city. The Union Square area at 14th Street and Broadway, which had long been an entertainment center, had seven moving-picture theaters. Because of their proximity, it is possible that immigrants were at least a small part of the audience in some of those theaters, a factor not reflected in the 60-percent figure. For example, in January 1909, a reviewer visited Keith's Bijou Dream on East 14 Street and remarked that the film shown, the story of a boy who leaves home for work in the big city, has various misfortunes "and returns home to find his mother dead...is a trite one, of course, but the subject was always a popular one with a mixed audience."[29] By "mixed" we can assume various ethnicities as well as social classes. Nineteen nickelodeons could be found on Second and Third Avenues, from 23rd Street to about 130th Street, much of which overlaps the working-class area described by Zeisloft. There were twelve theaters in Harlem proper, which was then a middle-class and lower-middle-class area.[30]

While 60 percent of the nation's most populated and lucrative film market (i.e., New York City) was a significant amount, it must be recalled that nationwide the working class represented about 70 percent of the audience. Despite its lack of cultural capital, that audience was providing most of the growth capital and could not be ignored by exhibitors. Nor, as we shall see, could its social and ethnic characteristics be overlooked by a middle class that aspired to gentility.

Allen has reviewed the studies of other historians (North, Grau, Sklar, Jacobs, Hampton) but could find little to explain the phenomenal growth of nickelodeons during this period. Hampton claims that the rise of the narrative film was directly instrumental in gaining new customers. This was certainly true in subsequent years, but in 1907 only 17 percent of the films typically shown were of a narrative type. Further, Allen points out that reports from vaudeville manager and trade paper fail to show a rise in demand that would account for the vast increase in actual moving-picture customers. The question is ultimately left unanswered, although Allen does mention that in 1909, in the nation's principal industries, "immigrants from Eastern Europe alone" represented at least a third of the labor force. While the number of narrative-type films jumped from 17 percent in 1907 to 66 percent in 1908, by that time nickelodeons were already well-established in working-class and business entertainment areas.[31]

I would suggest what seems dangerously obvious, that it was the rapidly-growing (and, until 1907, under-reported) immigrant population that fueled this growth, propelled by the experiences of the many at-first marginal operators who across the country opened small storefront theaters and, after counting the profits engendered nickel-by-nickel, opened theater after theater.

While the nickel price was within reach of many immigrants, the price was not then trivial. One observer, writing about his visit to a tenement theater in 1908, observed that

> perhaps the most interesting part of this human spectacle is the audience of wan and curious little people who stand outside, unable to afford the luxury costing five cents.32

Nickelodeons as Building Blocks

Many of the investors in neighborhood nickelodeons had first gotten their start in the business of peep-show penny arcades. A number of them, like Adolph Zukor, Marcus Loew and William Fox, would ultimately achieve considerable wealth and fame in the emerging industry.

Zukor, as a fifteen-year-old Hungarian immigrant, had arrived penniless in America in 1888 but by 1903, at age twenty, had managed to achieve some success as a furrier, and a had bank account of several thousand dollars. That year he happened to visit a penny arcade, managed by some friends of his, on 125th Street. Both Zukor and his fur-business partner, Morris Kohn, were impressed with the operation, which included peep-show devices and phonographs.

After studying the "box-office" figures, Zukor and Kohn decided to invest in their own arcade just off Broadway on East 14th Street,. The investment was not a small one. Over one hundred arcade machines had to be purchased and installed, including about forty peep-show machines and about sixty phonographs. The total cost came to $75,000. But, wrote Zukor, "from the beginning the enterprise was a success, the daily take ranging from five hundred to seven hundred dollars." When one considers that no attraction in the arcade cost a customer more than a penny, the figure stands as testament to the human traffic involved. By the end of 1903, the partners were opening arcades in Newark, Boston and Philadelphia, and both Zukor and Kohn had decided to sell off their fur business and devote full time to the arcades.33

At about this time, a friend of Zukor and Kohn, Marcus Loew, a thirty-four-year-old New York-born furrier and realtor, took note of his friends' success and invested in several of their arcades. Loew sought full partnership with Zukor and Kohn but was told there was no room for him. (This fact caused much mirth between Loew and Zukor decades later, when both had become fabulously wealthy and powerful in the movie business.)

The following year, Loew withdrew his investment from Zukor and Kohn and began operating a few storefront theaters. In 1905, aspiring to a better class of clientele, Loew opened in Brooklyn the Royal Theater, a refurbished former burlesque house ("Watson's Cozy Corner") as a small-time vaudeville house, offering live acts as well as moving pictures. By 1909, Loew had one of the largest small-time vaudeville circuits in the country, with twelve theaters in New York alone.[34]

William Fox and his family came to the United States from Hungary in 1880, when he was not quite a year old. He grew up in the poverty and teeming streets of the Lower East Side. As a child he sold newspapers, candy, stove polish (made by his father in their apartment), sandwiches and pretzels in Central Park, and by age eleven was a cloth cutter in a garment-industry sweatshop. Like many others, the boy worked twelve hours a day, six days a week, for a weekly salary of $8. After a number of years of saving every dime, he and a partner, Sol Brill, began their own firm, examining and shrinking cloth gotten from the mills. Their enterprise achieved a modest prosperity.

In 1904, Brill mentioned to Fox that a penny arcade at 700 Broadway in Brooklyn was for sale. After a visit to the arcade, Fox was sufficiently intrigued to buy it for $1,600, nearly his total savings. But business was poor; the former owner had hired "patrons" whenever he expected Fox to come. In desperation, Fox converted an apartment above the arcade into a moving-picture theater, hiring a barker to attract customers. The theater was a success, and Fox bought another theater--then another. Within a few years he owned fifteen theaters in Brooklyn and Manhattan and was making money hand over fist. Fox noticed, however, that the firms leasing or "exchanging" films were making more money than those exhibiting them, and in 1907 he formed the Greater New York Rental Company.[35] Five years later he would be the first of the film-distribution owners to challenge the Edison organization.

The same pattern of success that Zukor, Loew and Fox were experiencing in New York was true in other cities that had large immigrant populations. In 1906, Sam Katz. a fourteen-year-old high school student whose part-time job was as a pianist in a moving-picture house in Chicago, asked the owner how much his storefront theater made and was told "between three and four hundred dollars a week--net." The young man, mightily impressed, joined forces with Abe Balaban (who sang in accompaniment to song slides) and his brother Barney, to open a store-front theater. The place was a converted store, "with the marks where the shelves had been still decorating the walls." Used kitchen chairs or old benches served for seating. A wood stove provided heat.

Barney Balaban managed the business, while Abe sang during the program's song segment while Sam played the piano. By the end of Sam's sophomore year at high school, Balaban and Katz had earned enough money for expansion. They opened another storefront theater. When that proved profitable, they added another and another. On graduation day, when Sam Katz received his diploma, he was earning $400 a week.[36] Within a few years, the Balaban-Katz chain of theaters would be one of the largest in the country.

In 1906-1907, also in Chicago, Carl Laemmle, who would eventually found Universal Studios (and before that, have the distinction of being sued by Edison 289 times in less than three years) was discovering wealth through nickelodeons and would soon open his first film distributing operation. In New England, Sam Goldfish (later, Goldwyn) was achieving success as a glove salesman. Louis B. Mayer was finding that it was far more profitable to own movie houses than to deal in scrap metal. In Pennsylvania, Harry, Albert, Sam and Jack Warner, having failed at nickelodeon operation, were trying their hand at film distribution.[37]

At this point, none of these men were involved in film production It should be noted that all of them--most of whom were immigrants themselves and eager to escape their past--would quickly abandon the working-class nickelodeon audience in favor of the middle class, and would be among the first to build motion-picture "palaces." For, as film historian Robert Sklar has pointed out, they were thinking that if so much money could be made from the poorest citizens, "what could be made if everyone went to the movies?"[38]

While new fortunes were being made, the explosion in nickelodeons that began throughout the country in 1906 spelled doom for the traveling exhibitor. For these pioneers, who had introduced moving pictures to people in small towns and rural areas, it was becoming hard to find towns too small to have at least one nickelodeon.

Increasingly, showmen found that such town became fewer in number and farther apart, so that by 1913 only a few hardy survivors were left. In that year, when an Edison employee was asked about sales of a particular movie projector that had been a favorite of traveling exhibitors, he answered

Well, there were practically no traveling exhibitors left to buy it...formerly he could go into a little town and give an exhibition for a night or a week, whereas now he cannot find a town that has not got from one to half a dozen theaters in it, so there is no room for him.[39]

Formation of the Motion Picture Patents Company and the Rise of the Exchanges

In 1907, as a result of Edison's appropriation of Armat's sprocket device eight years earlier, and through relentless legal maneuvering and generous court interpretations of patent law, Edison was able to claim monopoly control of the American moving-picture industry. On March 7, 1907, the *New York Times* reported that the United States Court of Appeal had decided that

the moving picture apparatus of all the numerous companies in this country, with one exception, is an infringement on the patents covered by the Edison Company. For over four years litigation has been in progress over the use of the special sprocket movement of the Edison apparatus, which is the vital part of the moving picture machine. This allows the film that is being drawn through a machine to stop for a small fraction of time, say a thirty-fifth of a second, and no other means have yet been discovered that will answer the purpose.[40]

The "one exception" was the American Mutoscope & Biograph Company (formerly the American Mutoscope Company, William Dickson's old firm and soon to call itself simply Biograph), which claimed its own patents and had successfully fought Edison's legal actions since 1896. Biograph quickly formed its own licensee organization, the Biograph Association of Licensees, which operated under the company's own patents.[41]

Biograph's owners demanded Edison's acceptance of their patents as a prerequisite to their joining his combine, but Edison refused. The matter was not resolved until Biograph threatened to sell its cameras on the open market, licensing anyone who wanted one, a move that would have directly challenged Edison and caused exhibitors to take sides.[42] On December 18, 1908, the leading movie producers, including Biograph, announced the formation of the Motion Picture Patents Company (MPPC), later more commonly known as "the patents company" or "the Trust." It had acquired, by common agreement of the patent holders, all essential patents relating to the manufacture and projection of moving pictures. The members were the Edison Manufacturing Company, American Mutoscope & Biograph Company, Vitagraph Company of America, Kalem Company, Essanay Company, Selig Polyscope Company, George Kleine, the Lubin Manufacturing

Company, and two French companies, Pathé Fréres, and the George Melies Company.[43]

The MPPC was not formed as a producing company (although most of the members were producing films) but as a patent pool which issued licenses and collected royalties. From projector manufacturers, the MPPC collected $5 per machine. To use a projector, exhibitors were to pay $2 per week. Additionally, all producers, except Edison, were to buy their raw film only from the Eastman Kodak Company, with whom the Trust had an exclusive agreement, and to pay a royalty of one-half cent for each foot of film. Edison and Biograph owned most of the stock in the MPPC and were the primary beneficiaries of this agreement. For the other members, the principal benefit was surcease from Edison's lawsuits.[44]

By 1909, however, the *New York Times* was reporting that the Trust had so restricted exhibitors "in the selection of films that as matters now stand lessees of the machines can take only such film as The Trust sees fit to deal out to them."[45] The *Nickelodeon.*, a trade publication, reported a little later that year, that a number of "independent manufacturers, importers, renters and exhibitors from all parts of the country" had formed the Independent Film Protective Association, whose purpose was to "take aggressive action to sustain the open market and legal action against any monopoly striving to control the moving picture business."[46]

As the industry grew, fundamental changes, unrecognized as such at the time, were taking place. One of the most important was the new method of distribution that began in 1902. In that year, Harry J. Miles, an intinerant showman visiting the West Coast, noticed that in San Francisco David Grauman, an exhibitor, was buying a reel of film each week for several hundred dollars, to show in his theater, while in Oakland, just across the bay, Anthony Lubelski, another exhibitor, was doing the same thing. It occurred to Miles that if he bought a film for a hundred dollars and then rented it to exhibitors for fifty dollars, each exhibitor would save fifty percent, and every rental after the first two would be profit for him. In 1902, Harry and his brother Herbert opened the first film "exchange" in San Francisco, in the boarding house where Harry happened to be staying.[47]

Albert Smith recalled that the Miles brothers traveled across the country, "stopping at the small towns en route and making arrangements with the managers of theaters in these small towns to supply them with programs from week to week on a circuit basis."[48] A circuit was the city-by-city route a film followed before being returned to the exchange, with each theater manager forwarding the films to a predetermined address.

As competition increased in cities and towns, exhibitors found it necessary to change their programs more and more frequently, sometimes as often as six times a week. Obtaining fresh films was difficult, so many exhibitors, like William Fox and Carl Laemmle, opened exchanges just to guarantee their own supply.[49] Laemmle's example provides an insight to the profits to be made. His exchange, Laemmle's Film Service, founded in 1906, brought in receipts of $40 the first week of operation. A trade magazine in 1909 outlined what happened next:

> The second week he took in $90. By the end of the third week the receipts had grown to $250. Two months later his weekly receipts were $2000. Today his weekly receipts are $10,000, and the limit is beyond sight.[50]

It is suggested that the exchanges are significant to this study in that, through the exchanges and their relationship to exhibitors, the working-class audience was able to wield its influence and have its brief moment of authority. This was accomplished when film distribution was transferred from the producers (with their Victorian notions of what audiences should see), to local metropolitan exchanges which, by virtue of the quantity of film they ordered to satisfy working-class demand, also determined what was available to many exhibitors who were far from the cities.

As a matter of policy, the Trust would sell moving pictures only to "licensed" exchanges, those who paid a fee and agreed to sell only to licensed exhibitors. But the operators of many exchanges were less inclined to check the credentials of their customers, and this slippage (in addition to the huge profits being made by exchanges) was unacceptable to the Trust. In 1910, members of the Trust formed the General Film Company for the purpose of distributing Trust films. This firm sought to consolidate all of the exchanges under one organization, through the simple expediency of buying, "under threat of revocation of license," fifty-seven of the fifty-eight exchanges then in operation. William Fox, who owned the fifty-eighth exchange, refused, and determined to fight the Trust in the courts. He was aided by other exchange owners, including Carl Laemmle who declared his own state of war with the Trust.[51]

The Neighborhood Nickelodeon as Social Center

Unlike the vaudeville houses, with their high admission prices, the nickelodeon or storefront theater was nearby and cost only a few cents, rarely more than a nickel. Peg Bosworth, growing up in the small town of Franklin, Pennsylvania, recalled that at the town's first nickelodeon, The Pastime, "on Saturdays, if you went by one o'clock, children could go in for one cent. One penny."[52] The proximity of the theater, its appearance as a local enterprise, was important to local people who were reluctant to leave their neighborhood. The very smallness and shoddiness of such storefront theaters may have been construed as virtues that emphasized their friendly, informal, family-like atmosphere. This specificity of location is underscored by Frank LaMontagne, who remembered that in his town, there was advertising between films by local businesses. "They'd have a screen they pulled down with advertisements on the screen for the different merchants."[53]

Judith Goldberg points out that in 1908 *The Forward,* the Lower East Side's leading Yiddish newspaper, reported that "the immigrant population was flocking to the movie houses. For a nickel they could see a show, a dance and hear a song."[54] One writer observed that

> Certain houses have become genuine social centers where neighborhood groups may be found any evening of the week, where the 'regulars' stroll up and down the aisles between acts and visit friends.[55]

Audience activity was sometimes so spirited, in Jacobs' Bronx theater, on the southeast corner of Windover and Park avenues in the Bronx, that Mr. Jacobs had

> the assistance of a uniformed officer whose mission it is to keep order amongst the exuberant patrons of the house. The Bronx theater is situated in the thickly populated districts which appear to be prolific in small children of diverse nationalities.[56]

During this period the Bronx is often considered suburban middle-class territory, although the foregoing example implies that this was not necessarily so.

Both the social nature and the material conditions of the early movie-going experience are suggested by one Lower East Side resident who remembered the woman who first took her to the movies.

> To go to a movie in Europe, you have to get dressed if you gosomeplace, so she dressed up. The best jewelry she had years ago was a watch with a chain. When you had this on, you were all dressed. We go down. She paid a nickel each. It used to be a stable, and inside the smell was still there, and that was the movie, but still, she dressed up to go.[57]

The Forward, reporting in 1908 on the demise of the Yiddish theater during a time of economic depression, made special note of the social nature of movie-going, perhaps inadvertently revealing the apparent ease with which the customers assumed possession of the surroundings.

> The movies are not feeling the depression, for people must have entertainment, and five cents is little to pay. A movie-show lasts half an hour, and if it's not too busy, you can see it several times. They open at one in the afternoon, and customers, mostly women and children, gossip, eat fruits and nuts, and have a good time. [58]

In 1910, weekly attendance at movie theaters in New York was estimated at one-quarter of the city's total population of 1.5 million people. Nationally, 26 million people were attending nickelodeons every week, and three-quarters of all movie-goers were of the working class.[59] It was not only in New York that immigrants had converted their theater's spatial accessibility into institutions that suited their needs and customs. In Chicago, Jane Addams observed that an entire family could attend a picture show for a "small sum of money," and that "the five-cent theater is also fast-becoming the general social center and club house in many crowded neighborhoods." She noted that

> The room which contains the mimic stage is small and cozy, and less formal than the regular theater, and there is much more gossip and social life as if the orchestra and pit were mingled. [60]

Goldie's Theater, a nickelodeon in the mill town of Butler, New Jersey, quickly turned into a "social center." One reporter observed that Goldie's had

> A family patronage, and everyone knowing one another tends to make things sociable; during intermissions, the proprietors, Messers Goldie, are seen in the aisles, exchanging greetings with their friends. [61]

While walking through a New England mill town in 1909, Simon Patten, an economist, noticed that the schools, church and library were all closed. In contrast, Patten watched the throngs at the nickel theater.

> Here were groups of working girls--now happy 'summer girls'-- because they had left the grime, ugliness and dejection of their factories, and they were freshened and revived by doing what they like to do. [62]

In 1910, Byington studied ninety households in Homestead and acknowledged the importance of the moving-picture theater to the working class.

> Many people, therefore, find in the nickelodeons their only relaxation. Men on their way home from work stop for a few minutes to see something of life outside the alternation of mill and home; the

shopper rests while she enjoys the music, poor though it be, and the children are always begging for five cents to go to the nickelodeon. In the evening the family often go together for a little treat. [63]

That same year, Addams commented on the multiple lures of the moving-picture theater.

It is of access from the street...and the performance lasts for at least an hour; and, in some of the humbler theaters, the spectatorsare not disturbed for a second hour...The very darkness of the room, necessary for an exhibition of the films, is an added attraction to many young people, for whom the space is filled with the glamour of love making. [64]

Romance and Danger in the Nickelodeon

If "the space" did not always fulfill romantic fantasies on screen, Addams implies, the theater itself seemed to offer such potential. One of the ways by which this could be realized, is revealed in a letter to a trade journal in which an exhibitor complained that his projectionists, usually young men, constantly neglected their duties because "every girl who enters the place has an effect upon the running of the machine." In such circumstances, the projectionist would put on a "one minute intermission" slide, and use the time to introduce himself to the young woman. At a time when most projectors were still hand-cranked, the exhibitor commented that the way the projectionist could "grind up the reels toward the closing of the show when they have a date to keep is a marvel for rapidity."

One reporter noted that young males would often volunteer to be ushers just for the joy of seeing films for free (they were called "free ushers"). Under such circumstances, the reporter comments that the free usher "often wants some other things..." These "other things" included "the chance to pick up acquaintance-ship with young women through bestowal of the favors one in his exalted position has at his touch." [65]

Frank LaMontagne, from Northampton, Massachusetts, recalled that, in his days as a free usher.

in order to go to the movies...a friend of mine got a job in the Plaza theater on Pleasant Street, and he got me a job as usher, too, and we had to put on these jackets....And you know those jackets were never cleaned, and God, the backs of the necks were dirty. But in order to see the movies, instead of paying, I had to usher, for nothing. I mean, just to see the movie.

Mr. LaMontagne allowed that after a few days the movie got pretty boring, "But in order to see 'em for free you'd have to be on the job."[66]

These memories notwithstanding, "the glamour of love making," or the promise of romance, was implicit in the statements of several of the people interviewed. Ruth Meacham, growing up in middle-class Crestwood, New York, remembered that in the theater

> we were always young and lookin' for the boys, and the boys were lookin' for the girls, and there was the chance to get together. Giggling and stuff like that went on.[67]

Adelaide Jones remembered that she regularly attended the Saturday morning "kiddy shows" in Yonkers. When it was mentioned that attendance at these shows was usually predominantly male, Ms. Jones laughed and said, "Maybe that's why we went." The thing she remembered most clearly about her movie-going experiences was "my boyfriend holding my hand."[68]

Ruth Goldberg, also raised in Yonkers, remembered that her violin teacher played in a local theater, and because she had a crush on him, she would attend that theater as frequently as possible. (Her innocent affection for the teacher was still evident, more than seventy years later.) She recalleded a social ritual as she got a little older,

> ...more than teen-agers, a couple of men in the orchestra would take us out on Sunday night, when we graduated to Sunday night, see? First it was during the week, then later we went on Saturday and then, when we were really grown-up, we went on Sunday I forget who the other was. They both lived in New York. And they'd say, 'You wanna go out for something to eat after?' And we'd say 'yes,' and we'd go to the Chinese restaurant a couple of blocks away. And we never knew if they were married or not.[69]

In a trade publication, in 1908, an article warned theater managers that their theaters "should not be allowed to dwindle into trysting places," noting that there were "too many of the lower class taking advantage of the nickelodeon," it suggested that "the shrewd manager" would distinguish "the desirable person from another."[70]

One newspaper warned that school girls and women "go to see a moving picture, but they often see a good deal more than what's good for them."[71] The possibility of such experiences was undoubtedly one reason for middle-class parents to keep their children, especially their daughters, away from nickelodeons.

Addams pointed out that the

young people attend the five-cent theater in groups, with something of the 'gang' instinct, boasting of the films and stunts in 'our theater.' They find a certain advantage in attending one theater regularly, for the *habitués* are often invited to come upon the stage on 'amateur nights,' which occur at least once a week in all the theaters.[72]

Amateur nights featured local talent, and were another way "our theater" served to strengthen social cohesion in the community. This activity, however, was seen as anti-social by some critics. The fear of having children tainted by attendance in moving-picture theaters was such that in 1907 a Chicago city judge declared that owners of five-cent theaters who allowed young boys and girls to perform on amateur nights would be arrested and have their licenses revoked. The judge declaring this rule stated,

It may appear harmless to allow girls and boys to display their talent before an appreciative audience, but the influences are degrading. We expect to have several men arrested in a short time for allowing such things.[73]

With the *Chicago Tribune* leading the way, Chicago had been particularly anti-nickelodeon and was the first city in the United States to formally institute censorship of moving pictures.[74]

Behavior of the Working-Class Audience

The theater, whether as melodrama, opera, or other forms, had been a staple of life for many immigrants in their native lands well before the advent of movies, and many groups appear to have transferred their patterns of audience behavior to the new medium. A cartoonist caricatured the at-home behavior of audiences at a Yiddish theater on the Lower East Side

At the Yiddish theater they are hissing, and yelling 'Hurrah!,' 'Shaddap!' and 'Soda!,' some people read newspapers, a policeman with his billy club breaks up a fight as an elderly gentleman munches a big sandwich, and a man in the front row takes off his shoes.[75]

That food and audience participation were characteristic of the Yiddish theater experience is confirmed by others as well. "They brought Turkish halvah, Jewish bagels, farmer cheese--sandwiched into a newspaper; American fruit, Russian candy, something to drink," Harry Roskolenko, a resident, remembered.[76] Such behavior patterns were apparently carried over to the nickelodeon by Jews and other immigrant groups. Active conversation and food were frequently mentioned as characteristic of immigrant nickelodeon audiences. Edward Armitage, attending a working-class nickelodeon in Albany, New York, recalled that "a big thing there" was the baloney sandwich. The ritual involved stopping at a delicatessen, where "for a nickel you'd get a hard roll loaded with baloney. Plenty of mustard on it. That was a big part of Saturday morning movies."[77]

On the other hand, Ruth Meacham, growing up in middle-class Crestwood, New York, and attending the Bronxville movie theater in a "fairly high class neighborhood," thinks that sandwiches or food were prohibited. "I don't think we were allowed," she said. "I never remember eating. I don't remember that at all. Taking out lunch, or anything like that? No."[78]

At the theater, ethnic audiences had been less than passive. Roskolenko remembered that

> they carried on, equal in ego, as if they were the actors. Too often one could not hear the real actors, who were drowned out by the frightening comments.[79]

This responsiveness and tendency to interact with what was happening on stage, would serve immigrant audiences well in relation to motion pictures. For there was a considerable difference in the nature of the theater and moving-picture experiences for the immigrant spectator. Ethnic theater had been wholly comprehensible, in both language and context, to its audience. But for most immigrants, moving pictures, however fascinating, were in many respects a new medium in a foreign language, in a strange new world. The earlier middle-class audience, which had its own problems in learning to watch moving pictures, at least understood the nuances of the culture represented. The immigrants had no such advantage.

The evidence suggests that the habit of talking back to the actors was carried over into the nickelodeon, finding useful extension when individuals in the audience spontaneously asked questions regarding scenes that puzzled them, and other individuals just as spontaneously answered them.

Italians, whose own culture had a long history of active participation in local theater (particularly opera), embraced movies. Italy was a leading producer of films, and Italian actualities (those early short films that merely recorded an actual event or place, like a train arriving, a parade, or breaking waves) as well as comedies and dramas were common for all audiences, but most likely were specially selected by managers of theaters in Italian neighborhoods. One report, in 1909, mentions that in Newark, New Jersey, with a large Italian population "...[w]hen the earthquake in Messina was shown a few weeks ago lamentations in the Italian audiences were marked."[80] One observer noted how Italian mothers seamlessly blended churchgoing and child care with movie attendance: "Prayers finished, you may see a mother sorting out her own babies and moving on serenely to the picture show down the road." Also, for Italian women who lived alone, moving pictures were the preferred recreation.[81]

Long-time cultural institutions fell by the wayside, replaced by the new medium. Among Italians, neighborhood puppet shows had long been a popular form of communal and participatory entertainment. In 1910, however, one writer noted that Italians were beginning to lose these vestiges of their culture, lamenting the fact that they

> have permitted motion pictures to supersede their loved marionette shows, and where once these small imitations of real actors held undisputed sway, they are now seen no more... Newark, N.J., is an example of this change. It one time enjoyed the reputation of giving the best puppet shows in the country...now not a puppet show is left in Newark. Motion pictures have succeeded them all.[82]

For the immigrant, as for everyone else, film was still a language without rules. At least, whatever rules did exist (full figure, stagelike shots with very little editing) were constantly being broken. The medium itself required a certain degree of familiarity on the part of audiences before it could be fully comprehensible. Music helped bridge that gap. Silent films, from their inception, had rarely been silent. From the introduction of moving pictures in vaudeville houses, which often had full orchestras, to the most humble storefront theater, which usually had a piano or record player, music was part of the moviegoing experience. Only one of the people I interviewed could recall a movie theater that might not have had music, and several made special mention of music as a memorable part of viewing movies. Edison himself, it should be recalled, had originally considered motion pictures primarily as a supplement to his phonograph. In 1899, Henry Hopwood noted that when a motion picture of a boating disaster was shown (only thirty hours after the tragedy), it was accompanied by an orchestra playing "Rocked in the Cradle of the Deep."[83] Musical accompaniment not only helped suggest the mood of the filmed presentation, but also provided diversion and a form of continuity while reels were being changed.

For immigrants, who usually could not speak or read English, who rarely ventured outside their neighborhoods and who were therefore ignorant of many of the customs of their new world, movies became a means of negotiating the confusing and often threatening parameters of the broader social life. Nor was this effect limited to big cities. One Iowan reader of a trade paper responded to an article on the value of a lecturer by writing:

> Many a time I have watched a new film subject projected on the screen and thought to myself: if I only knew what this or that part of the picture meant, then I could get very much more out of the entertainment. [84]

Even "rube" films (those ridiculing the ignorance of rural types) could be seen as instructive--albeit exaggerated and amusing--warnings regarding the dangers of the city; they included subjects such as prostitution, pickpockets, drugged liquor, con artists and the like. In a film like *Rube and Fender* (1902), for example, how different was the rube in a big city who gets bowled over by the fender (or cowcatcher) of a passing trolley car, from the newly arrived immigrant? *Another Job for the Undertaker* (1901), by its title, demonstrated what happened when a rural visitor blew-out, rather than shut off, a gas light before retiring. Such a lesson could be valuable to working people who were familiar with candles but had not yet been reached by electric lights. [85]

Moving Pictures and their Reception by Women

The notion that in the nickelodeon women might "see a good deal more than what's good for them" can be viewed as a form of male protection of female virtue, as well as the subconscious defense of the male's own turf. Moving pictures had started out as a male entertainment. The first Kinetoscope parlors had been situated in business districts and largely patronized by men. The most popular subjects, like boxing matches and female exotic dancers, had been aimed at a male audience. Miriam Hansen has pointed out, however, that while moving pictures drew heavily from male-oriented spectacles, "the establishment of cinema as an institution hinged upon its appeal to an inclusive, heterosocial mass audience." Middle-class women discovered that movie theaters represented a liberating social space. They could go to movies on their own, without the necessity of a male escort and, once seated, could view physically active, adventurous heroines who were a far cry from the traditional ideals of femininity. [86]

Once moving pictures had been established as a singular attraction apart from vaudeville, we discover that, no matter where the theaters were located--whether in business and/or entertainment districts, tenements or the suburbs--patronage consisted primarily of women and children. Women found nickelodeons an inexpensive, convenient place to stop and rest during a day of shopping or after a day's work, and this practice was commented upon regularly in the press. "They say only women buy and read books, fill the opera-house and theater--also the film shows," wrote one observer. Wagenknecht, who grew up in Chicago, recalled that in those days "women would refresh themselves upon a shopping expedition by stopping in to see a film...." In 1908, F.C. Aikin, a vice president of the Chicago Film Exchange, noted that "the patrons of nickelodeons...are largely women and children."[87]

As evidence suggests, the motion-picture "vogue" was not exclusive to large urban cities and was beginning to influence traditional social patterns of behavior. A New Hampshire reporter observed a meeting of two Manchester women, loaded with bundles after shopping and obviously tired. One of the women suggested going to "the nickel" for a show, but her friend didn't understand what "the nickel" was. "Moving pictures," the woman persisted. "Come on, it's only a nickel." The friend said she really should get home to prepare her husband's supper, but the woman pointed out that her friend could prepare an even better supper after a half-hour's rest in the nickelodeon, "and off they trotted."[88]

The social realities behind this kind of reaction by women was made manifest by Ruth Goldberg, who grew up in Yonkers during the later stages of the nickelodeon era: she recalled a story her mother had told her:

> My mother used to tell me that before she was married there was a group of girls...about five of them, and always together, they always went to the movies on Saturday afternoon, the first show. They came out of that one, they went to the next one. And they would go until eleven o'clock at night. From one to the other. You know , they [the nickelodeons] weren't far apart. This had to be before 1911. And, a short time after they were married, my grandfather came downstairs one Saturday night, and my father was home from work, just sitting there. And he said, "Where's my daughter?" And my father said, "Oh, she went to the movies with the girls, they go on Saturdays. They come home at eleven o'clock at night." And my grandfather said, "Oh, really?" And he came down again when my mother came home, and he said, "Look, you're married now. And you don't do that. Your husband comes home and you're to have the dinner ready for him, on the table." Now that far back, who would ever think they would go to the movies and not be home to have dinner ready for their husband? Isn't that funny?[89]

Interestingly, some films were dealing with this very subject, in ways sympathetic to women. *The Tyrant's Dream*, a 1909 Selig-Polyscope film, told of "a tyrannical husband," who,

> returning home from work in the evening after a hard day's work at the office, finds his supper only in preparation instead of being ready

as usual, and in a rage abuses his frightened wife and her mother, who are making strenuous efforts to hasten the tardy meal and appease the wrath of their lord and master. [90]

The example of a group of young people "making the rounds" of moving-picture theaters was not an uncommon one. Writing about Harlem, one reporter mentions that parties

set out on what may be called a moving picture debauch, making the rounds of all the tawdry little showplaces in the district, between the hours of eight and eleven o'clock at night, at a total cost of, say, thirty cents each. They will tell you afterward that they were not bored for a minute during the entire evening. [91]

While newspapers, some magazines and the trade press made frequent and similar mention of this alteration of traditional domestic procedures, something beside respite from labor was occurring. Through moving pictures, women had regular access to forms of entertainment previously reserved for men. In 1907, in a trade publication, an article titled "Women and Prize Fights," while ridiculing the females' lack of understanding of the sport, nonetheless emphasized that women in considerable numbers did attend fight films.[92] Another reporter, a year later, discussed the film business in Indianapolis and commented on the ability of small nickelodeons to "take in money rapidly." The writer notes:

The pictures that drew the 'business' were those of the Gans-Nelson prize fight, and the notable features of the audiences was the fact that the women greatly outnumbered the men....[93]

Other accounts similarly report on the phenomenon of women attending fight films; the comments are usually derisive, which was to be expected. But at the same time they verify that women in large numbers were turning out to watch semi-nude men perform.[94] The films themselves usually show boxers wearing trunks that were little more than jockstraps, often more revealing than today's briefs, and nothing else but shoes, socks and boxing gloves. Male bathing suits at the time, for comparison, were two-piece affairs, with trunks reaching the knees.[95] Hansen has suggested that man's appropriation of the gaze ("the male gaze") actually began to erode with the advent of moving pictures that were attended by women.[96]

The appeal of this type of entertainment did not go unnoticed by producers, who responded with leading men in progressively scantier dress, reaching virtual institutionalization with Rudolph Valentino in the 1920s. What had begun as a liberating and broadening of experience for women rapidly became commodified and subverted.

4. MOVING PICTURES AND NICKELODEONS AS SOCIAL MENACES

The Middle Class Grows Alarmed

Meanwhile, exhibitors were simultaneously trying to satisfy their patrons, to wend their way through the precarious process of choosing between films produced by the Trust or by the independent producers who were springing up, and to manage their businesses. They were soon confronted by a new challenge, the growing perception in some quarters--that moving pictures in general, and moving picture theaters in particular--were a danger to the health and morality of the nation. Based on the evidence, it is likely that these charges, with the ensuing publicity and debate, discouraged many middle class patrons from accepting the medium. Their avoidance of the medium, I would suggest, ceded greater influence over film content to the very group whose presence (among other factors) was keeping the middle class out of nickelodeons--the working class.

The most serious charge against exhibitors was that the entertainment they were providing, as well as the spatial circumstances of the theater itself, were damaging to the morality of children and young adults. The darkness of the theater was considered to be evidence of its deviant and evil character. One study concluded that "an undoubted effect on standards of conduct" resulted from the fact that boys and girls were "packed in narrow seats, close together in a darkened room;" it warned that "mashing" and "knee flirtation" were becoming commonplace and that under "cover of dimness, evil communications readily passed and bad habits are taught." In addition, the study noted that nickelodeons were "favorite places for the teaching of homosexual practices."[1]

In Sunday services, priests denounced moving pictures and in 1909 the New York Board of Aldermen passed an ordinance that barred children under sixteen from attending moving-picture shows unless accompanied by an adult--an ordinance that was often ignored. *The New York Times* described in detail the activities of the Gerry Society, an agency dedicated to saving youngsters from the perils posed by moving pictures.[2] The society's goals were outlined by its superintendent, Thomas B. Walsh, who indicated that "properly conducted" shows were acceptable, but that the evil was in

> the dark room, filled with adults and children, absolutely without supervision, affording no protection against the evil-minded and depraved men who frequent such places...until irreparable harm is done.[3]

He reported that in the previous year the society had secured twenty convictions of "men who had lured children to their downfall."

In 1911, Maude E. Miner, Secretary of the New York Probation Association, quoted the confession of a child who had the "moving picture habit": "I always asked a man to get my ticket because I'm not old enough to go in alone," she was told. Ms. Miner commented, "It was not that the pictures were bad, but that the men took the children to the dark balcony, where they could begin their vicious work." She suggested that having brightly lit theaters would make such offenses impossible.[4]

As long as moving pictures had been displayed in respectable vaudeville houses to respectable middle-class audiences, they had not been perceived as a social problem. While religious groups and individuals would sometimes condemn films they considered scandalous, like *The May Irwin Kiss*, or a film that showed a bit too much female ankle or calf, the medium itself had not been attacked. But once nickelodeons had sprung up among the working class and in the most crowded areas of the city were rapidly growing in number, they were increasingly suspect.

Film historian Kevin Brownlow states it was the working class's exposure to, and interest in, the films about the Thaw-White scandal in 1906 that triggered the concern of the establishment. In that year the renowned architect, Stanford White, while dining in the theater on the roof of Madison Square Garden (a building he had designed), was shot to death by wealthy playboy Harry K. Thaw, who was irate because his wife, Evelyn Nesbit, had formerly been White's mistress. The great popularity of the several films depicting the murder (complete with White's infamous "red velvet swing" and "boudoir of a hundred mirrors") "obliged the establishment to take a new interest in the moving picture."[5] Often, the showing of those films was banned. In one Wisconsin city where a Thaw-White film was scheduled, the theater "was packed with an audience two thirds woman." As the film started by

> depicting an artist's studio the interest was intense. The exhibition got no further, for at this point the chief of police walked upon the stage and dramatically stopped the show.[6]

In New York, the People's Institute cautioned that moving pictures were "potentially too great an influence of popular attitudes to be left unsupervised.[7] A leading member of the Institute claimed that nickelodeons, "would not only appease the human craving for diversion to-day, but would inevitably shape the theatrical taste of tomorrow. Clearly, there was a duty to be done here.[8] Corrective supervision was necessary because, at the time, as Elizabeth Ewen has pointed out, "[m]oral philanthropy perceived poverty as a character flaw, a problem of bad habits or intemperate behavior," though correctable through adoption of the Protestant ethic--hard work, discipline, order, punctuality, temperance and "clean Christian living."[9]

In New York, the Board of Aldermen passed a resolution in 1907 calling for a "thorough report" on all the working-class venues for motion pictures, such as arcades, penny vaudeville, five-cent theaters, and moving-picture shows. The resolution noted that

> these places of public entertainment have caused much annoyance and vexation to residents in their immediate vicinity, prompting the general opinion that they are a common nuisance, because of the gathering of motley crowds and making loud noises and breeding fear of disturbance and the danger of fires....[10]

Sunday shows in Brooklyn brought angry responses from clergymen and "residents of fine houses," who denounced the "invasion of quiet residential sections of Brooklyn by moving picture men." When one exhibitor attempted to set up an "open air" picture show in a vacant lot on Bedford Avenue opposite the Union League Club, club members and neighboring property owners protested, on the grounds that the "location of a moving picture show at that point would bring an undesirable class of people into the neighborhood and that the value of property in the community would be seriously depreciated."[11]

On Christmas Eve, 1908, New York City Mayor George B. McClellan, feeling "personally responsible for the safety and lives of the patrons," ordered "each and every license issued by me for a moving picture show...revoked and annulled." Only quick action by several prominent showmen, who obtained a temporary injunction, prevented the losing of holiday receipts. *The New York Times* was moved to note, somewhat incredulously, that

> The moving picture theater has become so much a matter of course, that when Mayor McClellan moved a few days ago to revoke the licenses of such resorts in New York few realized what the industry meant in dollars, time and number of persons employed. [12]

A few weeks later a state supreme court justice declared McClellan's actions illegal. [13]

An editorial in the Birmingham, Alabama, *Herald* denounced "certain moving picture shows that for evil effects upon their patrons would put the saloon in the shade." Protection of female innocence, the paper claimed, was being threatened by these "cheap, common and vulgar" theaters which were, "almost exclusively, patronized by school girls and women who always have a loose nickel in their purse." [14]

The *Chicago Tribune* was an early opponent of moving-picture theaters that catered to the working class. While respectable vaudeville houses were considered acceptable, the inexpensive nickelodeons and storefront theaters were seen as hothouses of corruption. In 1907, an editorial in the *Tribune* announced that the Juvenile Jewish Protective League was the latest organization to come out against the "demoralizing effect" of the nickel theater, listed the major complaints leveled at the medium, and made a few suggestions regarding its continuance.

> Most of them are evil in their nature, without a single redeeming feature to warrant their existence.... They minister to the lower passions of childhood. They make schools of crime where murders, robberies and hold-ups are illustrated. The outlaw life they portray in their cheap plays tends to the encouragement of wickedness. They manufacture criminals to infest the streets.... Not a single thing connected with them has an influence for good. The proper thing for the city authorities to do is suppress them at once.... There should be a law absolutely forbidding the entrance to them of any boy or girl under the age of eighteen years... But the average five-cent theater does not have a single thing to commend it. Its influence is wholly vicious. It belongs with the lowest kind of dance hall, where the enjoyment of a popular form of entertainment is made subservient to the pandering to the basest passions of wicked men and women.... When an institution is everywhere recognized as evil in its influence it should not be tolerated for a day in the community where truth and honor and good citizenship is urged as worthy of the aspirations of childhood. There is no voice raised to defend the great majority of five-cent theaters because they cannot be defended. They are hopelessly bad. [15]

Less than a month after reprinting that editorial, *Moving Picture World* reported that Jane Addams of Chicago was going into the theatrical business, and, on or about July 1, would be opening a five-cent theater at Hull House. Addams, who was a prominent social worker and a strong advocate of publicly supported recreation for the youngsters of the working class, was clearly less intolerant of moving pictures. In 1899, she had cofounded Hull House, one of the first institutions of its kind; it was a settlement house dedicated to helping the immigrants who were streaming into Chicago in the late 1890s. Born a Quaker, Addams was a humanitarian and a pacifist, but a fierce advocate for a broad array of social causes, whose nature guaranteed publicity. A leader in the fight for women's suffrage and housing reform, she helped pass the first child-labor law and the first juvenile court.[16]

"Only attractive, amusing, edifying and moral pictures will be shown," the report continued. "The idea is to combat the influence of those five-cent theaters where pictures of a different character are displayed."[17]   But once the theater opened, Addams discovered what other exhibitors had discovered: that immigrants usually preferred the films that were not necessarily morally uplifting. Attendance at the Hull House theater was "disappointing," while other nickel theaters only a few blocks away were drawing crowds with films like *The Pirates, The Defrauding Banker, The Adventures of An American Cowboy,* and *The Car Man's Danger* .[18]

One of the most prominent and vocal critics of moving pictures was the New York Society for the Prevention of Cruelty to Children, which waged war against "the pernicious moving picture abomination." The Society was a powerful agent for dispensing anti-movie information, such as this excerpt from a report by the Society's Executive Committee, printed in the *New York Times*:

> Children support the picture shows at a cost to their little souls and bodies and minds that no one can compute....The child who steals her first 5 cents from home is already on the high road to destruction as surely as the simple girl who yields to the "kind" strange man who takes her to the pictures. The records of the Children's Court sadly prove that this new form of entertainment has gone far to blast the lives of girls and has led many boys to criminal careers. Boys have admitted to the Judges that their skillful housebreaking was suggested by these pictures.[19]

A school principal in Kansas reported that boys in his school had been discovered carrying revolvers, because they "wanted to brave [sic] like the heroes they had seen in the pictures in the five-cent theaters." Teachers on the East Side of New York City complained that movie attendance increased truancy. And in

Waterloo, Iowa, three preteeners attempted to steal jewelry because, they claimed, they wanted to imitate robbers they had seen in moving pictures.[20]

In New York, enforcement of the laws regarding children's attendance was usually left to the Society for the Prevention of Cruelty to Children. When unaccompanied children were discovered in nickelodeons, they were "gathered together by the Society's agents and conveyed to its headquarters in patrol wagons." The children were not punished, but held long enough to "put into them a fear of the law that will keep them out of the picture places...."[21]

As we have seen, from film's inception, laws prohibiting children from attending moving pictures had been tried in many communities with little success, but it wasn't until 1910 that an exhibitor actually went to prison. On July 12, the luckless William Michelson of 1503 Third Avenue, New York City, was sentenced to five days in City Prison and fined $500 for admitting to his theater children unaccompanied by an adult. (The fine could be avoided by serving an extra ten days.)[22]

Perhaps even more alarming to the upholders of social order, working-class audiences used moving pictures as catalysts for expressing viewpoints considered troublesome or alarming to authorities. An editorial in the Lowell (Massachusetts) *Sun*, criticizing objectionable pictures such as fighting roosters and bull fights, issued a warning. "But worse even than these was a picture of a labor strike in which one of the strikers killed the boss and won great applause."[23] Obviously, mere exposure to such inflammatory subjects was dangerous.

The era had been marked by conflict between labor and management, as workers attempted to organize unions. Chicago's Haymarket Square riots in 1886, in which a policeman had been killed by a bomb and scores of participants wounded, had not been forgotten. (As a result, three "anarchists" had been executed, although little evidence against them had been produced.) In 1892, a strike in Homestead against the Carnegie company had been met by the company's Pinkerton guards; in a twelve-hour battle, nine strikers and seven guards had been killed.[24] With labor unrest and imagined Bolshevism in the air, moving pictures as possible unleashers of the great unwashed were to be feared.

On occasion, these fears seemed to take palpable form. An aborted movie showing in the mill town of Torrington, Connecticut, in 1906, led one reporter to write

> This town was in the possession of a mob, owing to an attempt by a citizens' committee supported by the chief of police and the

prosecuting attorney, to prevent a moving picture show from giving a performance at the opera house.[25]

The authorities had stopped a Sunday movie exhibition attended by nearly a thousand people. According to one report, almost two thousand more people formed a crowd outside the opera house. Torrington's Citizen Committee had warned the exhibitors that any attempt to show moving pictures on Sunday would be stopped. The day before the proposed showing, the *Torrington Evening Register* predicted

> that there will be an exciting time in the neighborhood of the theater tomorrow night, particularly as everyone who buys a ticket is as liable to a fine as the ones who give the show.[26]

On the evening of the showing, six members of the committee attended the first performance, and "were hissed and jeered by the crowd." From the theater they went directly to the home of the town's prosecuting attorney, who dutifully made out two "John Doe" warrants which, in turn, were delivered to Chief of Police L. F. Hull. Chief Hull, accompanied by his deputies, proceeded to the opera house and arrested the ticket-taker and the projectionist. "No attempt was made to bring any charge against Manager Henry Aust," the *Evening Register* noted, "because the result of such a suit in a similar case last year showed that such an attempt would prove a failure." The story continued:

> The making of the two arrests stopped the show, and the demonstration began. The chief and his officers and the two prisoners werefollowed to the City Hall by the hissing and jeering crowd. Near the City Hall Chief Hull pushed his way into the crowd and took into custody Louis D'Amico, a young Italian who works at the Allen House. This angered the mob and sticks and stones were thrown. A missile which Chief Hull believes was a stone aimed at him struck D'Amico on the back of the head causing a painful bruise. Chief Hull turned his prisoner over to officer Demanche and drew his revolver and ordered the crowd to disperse, saying that if he were not immediately obeyed he would fire into the crowd. The mob took warning and withdrew. At about the same time several of the citizens'committee were discovered by the crowd in front of the Y.M.C.A. building; and the jeering and hissing began anew. Mr. Wilcox says that no missiles were thrown at him or his companion, but they that feared that the demonstration might result in violence, so they withdrew into the building. Later they were escorted to their homes by police officers.[27]

At a subsequent court hearing, the ticket-taker and projectionist were each fined $25, which was paid by theater manager Aust. The judge dismissed the case against D'Amico, "saying that no case was made against him."[28]

Torrington had seen immigrant Germans, Irish and Scandinavians populate the town during the first wave of immigration in the 1800s. During the second wave, beginning in 1890, large numbers of Slovaks settled in the town. Italians, the last and largest wave to arrive, constituted the largest segment of the population.[29]

If moving pictures could incite the working class, they could also "educate" and pacify them, and antilabor propaganda, in the form of simple narratives, was not uncommon. For example, *The Right to Labor*, produced by the Lubin company in 1909, is described as a

> sermon on strikes which deserves the consideration of every thoughtful man who may someday be called upon to decide whether he shall go with a crowd of agitators or shall choose the conservative course and stand by his firm.... the closing scene where Capital and Labor clasp hands and the angel of prosperity waves the olive branch above them, is well worth preservation as an inspiration to conservative action when any dispute of this character arises.[30]

The film's title came from a stirring scene in which the hero, John, crosses the picket line, declaring, "This is a free country. You have the right to strike. I have the right to labor."[31]

The Ringleader, a Pathe film, which dramatized "a phase of labor disturbances in France," nonetheless had a message for workers in America. In this film "a lazy worker is discharged" and incites his fellow workers to "strike and riot." A "faithful" employee is killed. At the man's funeral the workers "come to their senses and set upon the instigator and drive him away." The reviewer adds that the film's message "should not be lost on those who cherish the same views of employees and capitalists."[32]

The propaganda was not subtle. *The Benevolent Employer,* an Urban-Eclipse film, told of a generous employer who, when learning that any worker

> suffers from some particular ailment or malady he ministers to their wants. At noon he has luncheon served to them and later grants them leave of absence, and they go to a neighboring saloon to play cards. During the afternoon they threaten to go on strike and with difficulty are induced to remain.

The reviewer adds, "Whether intended or not, this film is wonderfully true to life."[33]

The fear of being overwhelmed by foreigners can be seen as the unstated impetus behind many calls for the broad interpretation and rigid enforcement of blue laws. For example, early in 1909, in New York, a mass meeting of clergymen and others interested in stopping moving-picture showings on Sundays, indicated that the "foreign element" were the principal lawbreakers, and suggested that Jews modify their religious beliefs by adopting Sunday as their Sabbath. "The Jew," the group resolved, "is not ethically justified in distorting the legal permission to labor on Sunday...into permission to conduct any amusement or other business on that day." The group, in an ironic counterpoint to the film discussed above, warned that "even now Hebrew businessmen are compelling Christians to work on Sunday."[34]

In view of the moving picture's reputedly destructive effects upon "young souls and bodies" and the work ethic, one would expect many parents to prohibit their children from attending moving picture theaters. Social and geographic data suggest that, while middle-class parents may have attempted to circumscribe their children's' attendance, immigrant parents were less likely to do so.

Middle-Class Attitudes toward Moving Pictures and Nickelodeons

Ruth Mezger, the daughter of a dental surgeon in Tarrytown, New York, recounted some of the fears of the day. She recalled sneaking off to an

> awful one, this nickelodeon, or something, they called it. It really was a fire trap. I went once--my father didn't know it. He wouldn't have let me go. In the first place you could have burned up.[35]

Edwin McIntyre, growing up in middle-class Jersey City, New Jersey, remembered seeing movies put on by the Methodist Episcopal Church, but pestered his uncle to take him to the neighborhood theaters. His uncle "didn't want to go, because he was a religious man and he felt it was sinful." To his family, "the theater and actors and actresses were associated with what was to them a decadent life."[36]

One Harlem resident recalled that until she was sixteen she didn't "know what a movie house looked like. My parents didn't allow me to go into a movie house because of their religion."[37] Growing up in New York, Miriam Cooper, who would a few years later be one of D.W.Griffith's stars, wrote that her mother would not let her go to the movies. "No nice girl's mother did. I only saw one movie before I started being in them."[38]

Raised in Astoria, New York, Gladys Cornwell remembered that movies were considered

> corrupt--even when I was twelve years old. They were considered off limits for refined people to go to. Almost as if you'd go to a bawdy show, or something.[39]

While not necessarily true of all nickelodeons, the general middle class viewed these theaters with great distaste. One writer noted that patrons feared finding themselves "wedged in between uncleanly people," and warned that this not remote possibility "militates no little against its patronage by decent people."[40]

In addition, the amount of interplay between immigrant viewers, the constant talking and explaining (one observer described it as "a running fire of explanations from the side lines"), babies crying, the spectacle of men spitting on the floor, as well as the odors of exotic foods and unwashed humanity, were just a few of the other factors that fueled the middle-class view of the moving-picture experience as vulgar and demeaning. Theater owners did what they could to discourage such offenses. Utilizing the intervals between films, many would project instructional slides on the screen announcing that "Somebody's baby is crying. Is it yours?" Or, "Don't spit on the floor...Remember the Johnstown Flood."[41]

One exhibitor, having visited a Lower East Side nickelodeon, complained, "I would have been more comfortable aboard a cattle train, than where I sat. There were five hundred smells combined in one."[42]

Being caught at a movie theater could be socially embarrassing for a middle class patron. A "lady correspondent" of the *Boston Journal* wrote that she enjoyed visiting moving-picture theaters occasionally, but that "curiously enough I have not confided my liking for this sort of thing to even my intimate friends." On one visit, she wrote, she was waiting in the theater lobby when she noticed someone next to her. It was

> "a woman friend of mine who seemed to shrink within herself when she saw me. She felt as I felt no doubt--like a child caught at the jam pot."[43]

George Cohen, a Trust exhibitor, testified that

> "One of the leading dentists of this country, told me last Sunday night that he had been ashamed to be going to picture shows in this country and only attended picture shows where he was not known."[44]

Sometimes more than one's reputation could be lost. In 1909, one writer, in Highlands, near St. Louis, reported "a very unpleasant experience" in a local theater. Two men had been sitting behind him, who "repeatedly disturbed the audience with the loudness and vulgarity of their remarks," and he discovered that when the show commenced and the lights disappeared, "so did my brand new Macintosh."[45]

On those occasions when permission was granted to children to attend a movie with their friends, middle-class parents would leave little to chance. Adelaide Jones, whose father was a businessman and boatsman, recalled that, even when young women attended moving pictures as a group, their "parents were always there to bring us home afterward," although street crime was relatively unknown and home was only a few blocks away, because "that's the way things were in those days."[46]

This was, after all, a time when a leading women's magazine, in its monthly column, "Good Manners and Good Form," was answering the question, "Shall a man and girl walk arm in arm?" with the recommendation that, while husband and wife sometimes did so, a man would offer such contact "in an emergency," and even then, "only in the evening."[47]

Magazine and newspaper writers usually reflected middle-class prejudices and racial fears, portraying the working-class moviegoing public in brutish terms. One western newspaper described the audience as

> of the lowest type. They have heads that rise to a peak and foreheads about an inch broad.... when someone is stabbed, or a horse falls in a bull fight, gored to death, their thick lips all seem to make sipping noises like a man drinking a luscious draft.[48]

A working class youngster growing up in rural Florence, a suburb of Northampton, Massachusetts, remembered that, although he would go to the movies whenever he could afford it, his opportunities were proscribed by local customs.

> "...our folks didn't want us out late at night. In fact we had to get home by nine o'clock, otherwise you'd get sent home by the police. They rang the curfew at nine o'clock, and all the kids had to get off the streets and get home."

If you didn't respond quickly enough. an officer would let you "feel the toe of his shoe on the bottom of your trousers."[49]

Data indicate that middle-class women's and family magazines, with a few exceptions, were in a state of denial regarding moving pictures and nickelodeons, in that both are rarely mentioned, despite the fact that the movies were spreading rapidly and becoming unavoidable. On those occasions when moving pictures are mentioned, it was usually disparagingly.

In the *Ladies Home Journal*. for example, there is practically no mention of the moving picture phenomenon from 1906 through 1909. Articles like "Seeing New York Through a Megaphone," which offered a tour of many neighborhoods and business and entertainment districts, and "The Strange Girl in a Large City," made no mention of moving pictures. In one article, "Out of Doors in the Holy Land," the author stated that his memory was as "vivid as in a cinematograph." Aside from this kind of passing reference, moving pictures were "invisible". In 1908, the *Ladies*

Home Journal was editorializing about the popularity of the theater among young women, emphasizing "salacious plays" and warning parents about "misdirected girls" acquiring the "matinee habit."[50]

In 1909, when *Ladies Home Journal* did address moving pictures, it was to issue a warning to its readers. An editorial, "They Saw Moving Pictures," citing some recently reported incidents, reported that a seventeen-year-old boy had

> sent a threatening letter to a wealthy man, demanding he leave $10,000 in a certain place at a specified time on pain of having his home blown up and his life and that of his fiancee taken. The boy was arrested and in court acknowledged his guilt and explained that the idea of sending that 'hold up' letter first occurred to him while seeing some 'Black Hand' pictures in a moving-picture show. The same week a fifteen-year old girl in Chicago stole some costly clothes from her mistress, ran away from home, and set out to seek "a knight of her heart in armor," as she explained she had seen a girl do in a moving-picture show.... Parents do not seem to realize the vicious influence of the pictures shown in the average 'moving-picture show,' but it is high time that they did not permit their children to attend these shows. [51]

Middle-class American families, as the prime audience for mainstream newspapers and magazines, were far more exposed and susceptible to the issues raised by these publications. Employment, with its exposure to more varied personalities and lifestyles, was not an option for middle-class women. Victorian patriarchal values dictated that their place was in the home. Most immigrants, on the other hand, could not read English or had trouble reading it, were cloistered in their ghettos and relied on their neighborhood's ethnic newspapers, which usually concentrated on local, more personal events. Moreover, in immigrant families, children were assuming roles of authority and independence undreamed of in traditional American families.

Immigrant Children as a Major Audience Factor

One of the observed truisms of Lower East Side life, along with the poverty, filth and overcrowding, was the conflict between the younger and older generations. The elders, uncertain in a new environment, desperately held onto their old-world religious beliefs and customs. For their children, such orthodoxy was embarrassing and too limiting in the face of the wonders and opportunities promised by the New World. One witness recollected that "there was scarcely a Jewish home on the East Side that was free from this friction between parents and children."[52]

Lincoln Steffins, on one of his frequent visits to the Jewish section, noted that we would pass a synagogue where a score or more of boys were sitting hatless in their old clothes, smoking cigarettes on the steps outside, and their fathers, all dressed in black, with their high hats, uncut beards and temple curls, were going into the synagogues... The sons were rebels against the law of Moses; they were lost souls, lost to God, the family, and to Israel of old...two, three thousand years of continuous devotion, courage and suffering for a cause lost in a generation.[53]

Mary Antin could see what was happening. "In Polotzk," she writes, "we had been trained and watched, our days had been regulated, our conduct prescribed. In America, suddenly, we were let loose on the street. Why?" Antin suggests it was because her parents, like many other immigrants, having renounced their faith in the name of being "Americans," had lost their system of ethics.

> My parents knew only that they desired us to be like American children, and seeing how their neighbors gave their children boundless liberty, they turned us loose, never doubting but that the American way was the best way. More than this, they must step down from their throne of parental authority, and take the law from their children's mouths; for they had no other means of finding out what was good American form.[54]

Antin recalls that, upon joining her father in the New World, she was almost instantly warned not to behave like "greenhorns," and was given strict instruction on avoiding such behavior.[55] For many an immigrant parent, movies must have seemed as American as the Statue of Liberty and therefore had to be good.

In addition, for single immigrant women, unlike their middle-class counterparts, necessity dictated that they had to work. Belle Mead, in commenting on the tendency of young Jewish women to go to work, noted;

> She then becomes as independent as her brother and both are influenced by their contact with the commercial world, new ambitions and the chance for freedom. The old traditions lose ground.[56]

One immigrant described what he saw: "A Godless country, America. All the wrong side up. The children are fathers to their fathers, children to their children." Erik Erikson, the sociologist, noted that immigrant children became "their parents' cultural parents."[57]

Italian parents encountered similar pressures. Ida L. Hull, a social worker, observed that,

> like all children, the Italian child tends to follow the crowd. He soon wants to go to the movies, or hike to the country, to join in all the amusements of his companions. It is the thing to do in America.[58]

Unless one was familiar with the rigid control exercised over youngsters in the typical Italian family, one observer noted, it was difficult to "understand what a stride toward independence the Italian girl has made by simply working in a factory, instead of at home."[59]

The effects of this new freedom could often produce both cultural disorientation and exhilaration, in the person being thus liberated. Maurice Hindus, a Russian immigrant decided at the age of fifteen to leave the suffocating confines of the Lower East Side and find employment in a real American "town." He found work, at $15 per month, as a farmhand in Mount Brookville in upper New York State. Becoming acquainted with farm children his own age during this experience, he encountered his first American party, including the game "Spin the Platter" (identical in result to "Spin the Bottle"), which he refused to play, because

> I was too overcome with bewilderment, for never had I seen anything like it in the old village. Boys and girls kissed at dances, at spinning socials, at *nochleg*, with no show of promiscuity and no search of a collectivized justification for the indulgence. Never should I have imagined that the sons of Elder Jepson's Baptist church would lapse into such fervent awareness of 'the pleasures of the flesh.' Yet here they were proclaiming this awareness with untrammeled, almost boastful delight.[60]

Experiences of this type, which continually challenged Old World customs, contributed to the "worldliness" of immigrant children and further diminished parental authority.

Sometimes, even cheating your mother's customers could be interpreted as image-enhancing as well as economically instructive. Roskolenko remembers that (about 1915) as a youngster on the Lower East Side and working at his mother's newsstand, he would shortchange customers by about six cents a day, and use the ill-gotten gains for entrance to the Harry Howard Theater, near Clinton and Grand streets. Usually, when the show was over, patrons would have to leave, unless they had a "late pass," a cardboard pass issued to people who had come in the middle of a show. Roskolenko recalls the material conditions of this "two for a nickel" theater, as he describes his own adaptive behavior.

> Since all this was done in the dark, it was very easy to palm off a piece of cardboard torn from a crackerjack box as a late check--and to stay on in this crowded, dismal, foul-smelling arena for a repeat of Hollywood heroics...Usually my initial entry used only two of my six cents. For I would stand outside of the movie house as the show began and yell, "Who's got three cents? I got two." It might take me a while to find someone with three cents, a kid who would insist on holding the late check if we came in during a show--after all, he'd paid a penny more than I had. When the boy decided to go to the toilet,

I'd demand the late check in the event that he found a friend and never returned.... This was my first vague, private economic planning and training.[61]

In New Britain, Connecticut, Reverend Herbert Jump, the pastor of a local church, surveyed students to "ascertain the vogue of the moving picture." Three hundred and fifty "scholars," from ten to fourteen years of age, were interviewed. The study showed that three hundred and sixteen (90 percent) went to the movies. One hundred and eighty-three (52 percent) went once a week, forty went twice or more a week, six went six times a week, and nine went every day. (Of the last group, three had jobs in a movie theater.) New Britain, known as "hardware city," was a factory town.[62]

Based on available data, there can be little doubt that both middle-class and working-class children were attracted to moving pictures. But the social and cultural circumstances alluded to meant that immigrant children had more freedom to attend moving pictures, while middle-class children were not allowed to attend as frequently.

Unsafe, Overcrowded and All Seats Filled

As noted, attacks upon moving pictures converged around two issues: (1) the immoral and anti-social content of the films themselves and (2) the dangerous and unsanitary nature of the neighborhood theater.

The perception of danger associated with these two problems was inflamed by social, religious and reform groups for a multitude of reasons, not all of them without reasonable cause: The nitrate film used by filmmakers was unstable and highly inflammable, with a combustion point of 284 degrees Fahrenheit. Reels of film could and did burst into flame in theaters. In 1907 the Dreamland moving picture theater in Chattanooga, Tennessee, "was totally destroyed by fire...being the second local enterprise of this kind to be destroyed since the craze began." The fire had been caused by a careless projectionist, who allowed "the light to play too long on a picture film."

The projection machines, too, could be dangerous. "That was what we were all desperately afraid of," Wagenknecht recalled. "The machine might blow up at any minute." And such catastrophes did occur. In Kankakee, Illinois, a projector exploded in a nickelodeon and threw a thousand spectators "into a panic, during which many women fainted and were trampled upon." Fortunately, "no one was injured seriously." This physical problem, however, was relatively easy to solve.

Projection booths, rather than simple stands or tables, were set up. Booths were generally made of steel and asbestos to enclose the projector and film and prevent the spread of fire, should it occur. While this caused great discomfort for projectionists (the booth interiors got uncomfortably hot), at least the public was protected.[63]

In 1908, a study of one hundred and eighty "places where these moving picture machines were operated," revealed that over 90 percent were "kept by foreigners and incompetent people" who could not read or understand the printed instructions for operating the projector. More rigorous training for operators was suggested.[64]

Crowded and unsanitary conditions were less easily solved. In 1911, New York City's Office of the Commissioner of Accounts studied these problems; it was pointed out that, because theaters holding three hundred or more people had to comply with city requirements, most theaters were constructed to hold fewer than that number. "There are at the present time approximately 450 motion picture shows in Greater New York under a common show license," the report stated, "and 290 under a concert or theatrical license. Of the total number, approximately 600 are constructed with a seating capacity of under 300." The report mentioned that anyone wishing to operate a moving-picture theater had to deal with seven departments of city government: the Health, Police and Fire Departments, the Bureau of Buildings, the Department of Water Supply, the Mayor's Bureau of Licenses, and the Tenement House Department. Bureaucratic obligations notwithstanding, the report cited the conditions found during an inspection of fifty theaters selected at random in Manhattan, Brooklyn and the Bronx:

> Generally speaking, the conditions found to exist are such as attach to cheap and impermanent places of amusement, to wit; poor sanitation, dangerous overcrowding, and inadequate protection from fire or panic. Of the fifty places examined, 36 were crowded; in 20 the ventilation was poor, and in 17 positively bad; in 31, children under the age of 16 were admitted unaccompanied by parents or guardian.... As stated above, the majority of 50 places examined were found to be badly overcrowded, in some instances, indeed, the aisles completely blocked by standing spectators, so that it was impossible for our inspectors to force their way into the hall. The ventilation in most of the places was wretched, no air being admitted, except as such as came through the front doors. In many places attendants went through the room with an atomizer, spraying perfumery on the crowd to allay the odor....[65]

The inspectors noted the following comments about specific theaters:

> Third Avenue, Manhattan: This is a vile smelling place....
> Fulton Street, Brooklyn: All seats filled and standing in the rear were 61 persons completely blocking the aisles. As a matter of fact, including the persons standing there were 373 people in attendance at

the time of inspection, and a panic or fire could not but have resulted disastrously.

Pitkin Avenue, Brooklyn: All seats filled and every available bit ofstanding room, including the aisles, crowded. In most cases, five, six and seven persons were occupying three seats between them, some sitting in laps of others. Children under 16 were freely admitted unaccompanied. No attempt was made to maintain order. Quarrels were frequent. An alarm of fire would have resulted in many fatalities. A detailed inspection impossible on account of crowd.

Pitkin Avenue, Brooklyn [presumably different from preceding]: Seats full and about 250 standing in the rear and in the aisles. A critical inspection of this place was impossible. The crowd was surging back and forth, pushing and shoving for vantage points of view...the air was fetid and stifling.... This place was without one redeeming feature. [66]

Such reports were not necessarily perceived by the exhibitors as negative. The most common opening phrase for each theater studied is "All seats filled," and it would have been an altruistic exhibitor indeed who construed this as bad news. Further, it is self-evident that the public alluded to did not find the theater conditions objectionable enough to stay away. From what we know of immigrant audiences, it is entirely possible that the social behavior and conditions they most enjoyed (crowded, boisterous, people sitting on laps, with no one to "maintain order"), were precisely what was unacceptable to middle-class authorities, who did little to alleviate the considerably worse conditions that represented living reality for most of the working class.

In 1909, the Trust, located at 80 Fifth Avenue, was doing everything within its power to quell the flood of charges being leveled at the moving-picture industry. The Trust's management invited the city's most prominent social activists to a meeting, whose purpose was to "pass on the propriety" of the Trust's films and to insure that "no evil seed shall be dropped into the young mind from these pictures." Among the attendees were Judge Charles Sprague Smith, founder and president of the People's Institute, a progressive organization that considered leisure an important factor in the fight against crime, Reverend Walter Laidlaw of the Federation of Churches, Thomas McClintock of the Society for the Prevention of Crime, Gustav Strabenmuller and Evangeline Whitney of the Board of Education, and Miss Theresa Townsend of the Women's Municipal League. [67]

The Trust, the public was assured, would supply only films that were "above reproach," and would withdraw licenses from any theaters that were not in "safe and sanitary condition." Decisions made by the Trust could have far-ranging impact; it was pointed out that the Trust supplied films to about one hundred film exchanges across the country, who in turn supplied about 5,000 theaters. The meeting attendees formed a "temporary board of censors" and "labored for five hours, inspecting 18,000 feet of pictures." Only about 400 feet were actually condemned, including *Every Lass a Queen* "because it was inartistic."[68]

Because of its monopolistic position, the Trust had the power to enforce its policies, which required clean and comfortable theaters so as to "end the day of the moving picture room," as well as "educational, moral...cleanly amusing" films.[69]

It seems, however, the Trust's insistence upon films they perceived as of the highest moral character was not commensurate with what many exhibitors felt would fill their houses, and this disparity of perceptions, based largely upon what the working class preferred, was a growing source of conflict within the organization. As more and more theaters were bought up by the lower-class entrepreneurs from Eastern Europe, these businessmen, who were responsive to their audiences' preferences and less inclined to "uplift" them, exerted increasing pressure for the production of less "proper" films.

5. THE POWER OF THE METROPOLITAN NICKELODEONS

The Plight of the Out-of-City Exhibitor

Despite the phenomenal growth in nickelodeons throughout the country, the situation in 1910 for the rural or suburban exhibitor who was dependent upon metropolitan film exchanges was complicated by the needs of working-class audiences. Smaller exhibitors, especially those located in towns far from the cities, and who considered that their patrons were culturally different from immigrant city folk, were finding it difficult to obtain films suitable for their audiences. One outraged suburban exhibitor complained in a trade magazine about the causes of the mistreatment he had been subject to, coincidentally describing the overall situation.

> The East Side exhibitor has had altogether too much to say in deciding what the public wants and what it does not want. He has practically dictated the policy of the film exchanges in New York. The East Side Exhibitor is so numerous that he forms a commercial factor too important to be overlooked by the renter. He holds the balance of power in the New York exchange.... this influence is felt far from the city. The New York exchanges supply out of town customers who cater to an intelligent educated trade. These rural exhibitors can obtain only such film as approved by the East Side exhibitor, because the number of moving picture houses in that district is so great that it outweighs every other section that looks to New York for its film supply...[1]

Within this statement of protest the exhibitor confirmed that the working-class audience, through the exchanges, had a pervasive influence over film content, an influence not acceptable to a refined, "educated" audience. To underscore this point, the writer described a visit to an unnamed Lower East Side nickelodeon: he came to this conclusion:

> But what is hardest to swallow is that the tastes of this seething mass of human cattle are the tastes that have dominated, or at least set aside, the standard of American moving pictures. [2]

Just what "standard" the exhibitor was referring to is unclear; D.W. Griffith had started making films for Biograph in 1908, and these were greatly appreciated by immigrants. But aside from its value as evidence of the working class's influence, the letter is informative on several levels: It serves as a possible example of what the average exhibitor had to contend with, just to be assured of getting films appropriate for his audiences; this demonstrates the growing power of the film exchanges, a

The "Retail Department" of the Empire Film Company, at Broadway and 55th Street, in 1910. Films could be rented or purchased here for showing in theaters.

reality that producers, too, were well aware of--and which would propel them towards the outright ownership of the means of production and distribution. The letter also displays the then common view of the immigrant audience as a stupid, barely human mob. But the audience and the exchanges aren't the only targets. A certain type, the "East Side exhibitor," is specified. While this could be interpreted as "immigrantphobia," it is more probably a veiled reference to the many Jewish theater and exchange owners, such as Loew, Fox and Zukor, who were building huge theater chains primarily, though not exclusively, in New York.

Another example of both contempt for immigrants and of anti-Semitism in regard to exhibition appears in a reporter's analysis of the origins of immorality in the moving-picture business. The reporter writes that he looked out of his window and, beholding the Statue of Liberty, reflected upon the rule that "liberty is not license."

> There was time when the 'riff-raff' of certain parts of Europe, hearing that America was a 'Free Country' governed by 'Liberty' which in their blind ignorance they supposed to be license, hurried to the 'Land of the Free' in droves; Anarchists, Nihilists, Black Hands and everything else; for in America could they not 'do as you please'?.... We all know that even as 'men rush in where angels fear to tread,' and as 'undesirable citizens' rushed to these shores, so many 'undesirables' rushed into the moving picture business and by their undue 'License' did much evil.[3]

While anarchists, nihilists, and the Black Hand are cited as particular examples of immigration excess, they are incidental to the reporter's real complaint. None of these groups were known to be connected with the moving-picture business. The "riff-raff of certain parts of Europe" certainly didn't apply to the upstanding gentlemen of the Trust. That description fit only the certain "East Side exhibitors" referred to previously, and again signifies anti-Semitism and the middle class's fear of immigrants' influence.

Anti-Semitism was far from unusual, but in fact could be expected as fashionable among Anglo-Saxon businessmen. The Trust itself was virulently anti-Semitic, which is particularly ironical in view of the mythology that Jews started the movie business. The only Jew among the original Trust movie manufacturers was Sigmund Lubin, of the Lubin Company. Trust film producer William H. Swanson testified that he was told by George K. Spoor, one of the Trust's founders, that they "were going to dispose of Lubin in their own way, that is, that Mr. Lubin would be disposed of eventually, but they did not know just exactly how it would be done." Swanson recalled he had numerous conversations about Jews with Trust members and executives, including Frank L. Dyer, Edison's personal attorney, who told him that "there would not be any room in the moving picture business for the Jews," a statement that must rank with history's most inaccurate predictions.[4]

A trade-paper reporter reminded his readers that

> most of the shows of the big cities are run by men who came to this country, the land of the free, believing they could do anything and

even violate the laws, consequently they do not care what they show, and they do not care about the morals.... [5]

One exhibitor complained about his competition, "a lot of unscrupulous, greedy exhibitors," described as former "peddlers, hucksters," who, after ruining the business for everyone, "will return to their vocation of selling shoestrings or vegetables."[6] The general middle-class view was captured by exhibitor H. F. Hoffman in his article "A New Race of Degenerates," in *Moving Picture World* in 1910. Hoffman described film exchanges during their "crowded hour," from eleven o'clock to twelve noon. He stated that, while movies had been blamed for many things,

> so far they have escaped the blame for producing a new race of degenerates, namely the city 'operator.'.... Bear in mind that not every person seen in a film exchange is a member of this race. Few ordinary mortals are obliged to mingle with them for an hour each day, but not by choice.... It is difficult to describe in a word the full characteristics of any one specimen of the degenerate operator. Two words might do it: greasy and smutty. Greasy of body and smutty of mind. .... The members of this race are never named such names as James or John or Frank or Edwin. They have special names of their own. such as 'Bughouse,' 'Spaghetti,' 'Muzzletoff'....[7]

Assuming the accuracy of this obviously bigoted description, it is easy to see one appeal of these exchanges over the Trust's more "respectable" operations. Most small nickelodeon and storefront-theater owners were uneducated, working-class people themselves, many of them immigrants. It is not unlikely that they preferred dealing with Muzzletoffs and Spaghetties rather than with James, Johns and Franks.

The Exhibitor As Impresario

One of the questions raised in this study is this; Did a local exhibitor recognize the particular preferences of the audience and if so, was he able to adapt presentations in his particular neighborhood theater to satisfy them? While much of the following material involves the audience's behavior, its primary significance is in the reactions and subsequent responses of exhibitors in regard to immigrant preferences, which is thus being included here.

Testifying in the United States Government's suit against the Trust in 1913, Louis Rosenbluh, the manager of a film-rental company, was asked whether the tastes of different communities varied and whether the patrons of a theater in one section of New York would prefer films different from those popular with the patrons in other sections. Rosenbluh answered that that was certain, and then provided examples from the ethnic working class.

> The Italian population or Hebrew population, and the people who are living in the more crowded sections, they seem to care more for the dramatic subjects, and a certain amount of western shooting and western scenes and cowboys.[8]

He contrasted this to the supposedly more genteel tastes of the middle-class vaudeville/movie-house audience.

> Some of the best known theaters that we are supplying at the present time, theaters seating 3000 people at a time, do not want to show a Western or cowboy feature. The patrons absolutely object to looking at pictures of that kind, and we were in fact notified by the managers of these theaters to exclude from their program anything of that nature. Do not like anything with the stabbing or killing, whereas in the lower classes or sections, the crowded sections, they just eat it up.[9]

One movie exhibitor was asked whether the popularity of his shows depended on "novelty, originality and artistic excellence." He answered;

> It depends largely on the temperament of your audience, and just where your theater is located. Now, I find that in certain locations, in lower Jersey City [predominantly Italian], that there is a class of people there who like things that are, well, savoring of great excitement, and action. They like cowboy pictures, and hold-ups, and bandits, and things of that kind.... [Exhibitors] know they have to vary their programs in order to satisfy the different tastes of the public. And I know just what I have got to give my congregation over there in Jersey.[10]

It was within the power of the exhibitor to customize a presentation to fit the precise tastes of the audience. For metropolitan exhibitors, at least, a tremendous variety of films was available in every conceivable category of interest. Those exhibitors, in fact, had firm control over the content, pace and duration of any presentation within their theaters. The exhibitors could select the films to be shown and determine what types of films best satisfied their audiences. Choices were wide, and ranged from *The Wonders of Nature,* to *The Wright Brothers' Aeroplane*, and *Manufacturing Nail Heads*, as well as comedies and five-minute dramas.[11] With a pair of scissors, the exhibitor could easily remove unwanted sections of film and could, if need be, change a film's title by merely splicing on a title taken from another film. Jack Warner claimed he did this with almost reckless abandon while trying to fill orders for the family's film-exchange business.[12]

Despite the evidence presented, there is reason to suspect the validity of claims that there was a difference in the type (genre) of films preferred by audiences of various classes. Reportedly, the middle class enjoyed educational and scenic films, while the working class enjoyed broad comedy and action. A claim could be made, however, that for middle-class sensibilities the educational and travel films were the only aesthetically acceptable films, given the then prevailing scenario and the technical levels of comedy and action films. Later, when product had been somewhat refined through the efforts of filmmakers like Griffith, Walsh, Chaplin and DeMille, middle-class audiences would find themselves, along with the working class, in common acceptance of comedy and action films.

Taking advantage of neighborhood cohesion and pride, but at the same time contributing to it, some exhibitors arranged for the photographing of local events, to enhance box office receipts. In 1908, a writer for *Moving Picture World* noted that

> Some nickelodeon managers have figured that moving pictures of some big local event will double and sometimes treble their receipts for a week, and they have offered to very generously contribute to the expense of securing them. [13]

The writer mentioned that he knew of a company that had spent a thousand dollars preparing local views and whose "share for the week the show played the place was almost three thousand dollars."[14]

Exhibitors could arrange isolated filmed scenes so as to offer a form of continuity. For example, during the Spanish-American War, one exhibitor showed *The 71st Regiment of New York* on parade before leaving for Cuba, then showing the arrival of troops in Tampa and their departure to the front. The next film, *Thrilling War Scene*, showed the American flag being defended. As Musser points out, both films had been ordered separately; it was the exhibitor who created the continuity. The Eden Musee usually constructed its film programs around a single subject, such as "Scenes in and around Key West and Tampa, Florida."[15]

In addition, exhibitors could plan special nights. The *Forward* reported that

> The movies have candy nights, grocery nights, and chicken nights. At intermission the audience draws lots and the lucky one win a present. You can pay a nickel or a dime and go home with a whole chicken. [16]

Hansen has pointed out that this freedom on the part of exhibitors made each of these early shows more like a live performance than a "uniform product." Furthermore, the exhibitor had other means of arranging for variety, including song slides, and magic lantern and stereopticon shows.[17]   In 1908, *Moving Picture World* was suggesting to exhibitors that "where the management cannot afford a two-reel show, the travelogue recommends itself. Sets of slides, with brief lectures are now obtainable for rental and at very low rates."[18]   In 1909, every issue of *Moving Picture World*, had a section called "Slide Notes," which shared anecdotes and provided technical advice for preparing and projecting slides. This assortment of entertainment variables, with moving pictures as their hub, made each local exhibitor an impresario of sorts, capable of satisfying the particular tastes of the neighborhood's audience. This, combined with the explanatory discourse that arose spontaneously throughout the audience, positioned the neighborhood theater as a vital extension of the community itself, and provided the educational and social space that was desperately needed by the urban working class.

This versatility of presentation is only remarkable in comparison with what was to follow. Subsequent film and exhibition practices--longer, more engrossing films that called for silent attention, along with theater palaces with uniformed ushers to maintain order--would gradually cater to a mass audience. Thus, the exhibitor's ability personally to tailor film programs so as to accommodate a neighborhood audience's preferences would be greatly diminished.

Middle-Class Theaters in the Age of the Nickelodeon

An example of middle-class movie exhibition in 1906 is provided by the travel-lecture forms of presentation, as exemplified by Burton Holmes and his "travelogs," a word coined by Holmes in 1904. Holmes had begun his lectures in 1891, using projected slides as visuals, but switched to moving pictures in 1897, when he formed the Burton Holmes Corporation. Holmes would usually accompany his slide and film presentations in person, but discontinued this practice when Paramount Studios became the distributor of his films in the 1920s.[19]

An issue of a suburban daily newspaper, *The New Rochelle Pioneer*, in 1906, displayed ads that illustrated similar forms of middle-class presentations. One advertisement announced that "Collier's war correspondent, Mr. Robert L. Dunn will exhibit 1-quarter million dollars actual battle scene pictures." An accompanying article, captioned "How Russia Lost," stated that the lecture would explain how

> millions of money, hundreds of thousands of men, an entire navy and national position and honor were lost by Russia in the recent [Russo-Japanese] war. If you wish to know why, go to the lecture of Robert L. Dunn...[20]

Prices were listed as fifteen, thirty-five and fifty cents, "which includes telescopic slides," --and thereby precluded a working-class audience. On the same page an ad offered a Saturday program (matinee: 2:15, evening: 8:15), of "Archie L. Shepard's Moving Pictures." The ad assured the reader that the films would be from Shepard's "finest collection of high class moving pictures," and would include "a personal visit to the Sphinx and Pyramids of Egypt...among the many pleasant surprises." Matinee prices were ten cents for children, twenty-five cents for adults; evening admissions were fifteen, twenty-five, thirty-five and fifty cents. Shepard was an exhibitor who rented space and provided hour-long shows of films in the midwest, New England and New York.[21]

Similarly, on any given day in 1908, the entertainment pages of New York City's newspapers revealed a rich variety of venues for the middle class's consumption of moving pictures, although many of them were part of a vaudeville program. In January, Burton Holmes "began his annual series of travelogs at Carnegie Hall." Both still and moving pictures were employed, "which created a profound impression because of their beauty."[22] In Manhattan, the Columbian theater advertised "matinees daily, 15c, 20c, 25c. Evenings 15c, 25c, 35c, 50c." Shepard's moving pictures, however, were only an "extra attraction" along with the stage melodrama. At the Majestic, "Brooklyn's perfect theater," Lew Dockstader and his minstrel show were appearing in addition to "Liberty Moving Pictures."

The Bijou Dream (formerly Koster & Bial's), on commercial 23rd Street, was advertising its all-film exhibitions of Pathé Fréres films and the "wide variety of subjects represented," while Blaney's Lincoln Square theater, at Broadway and 66th Street, also offered matinee and evening performances of Pathé Fréres' moving pictures. In the more ethnically and economically diverse uptown area, the Harlem Opera House advertised "the world in motion," with "European and domestic films of Every Day Life."[23]

The prevalence of European films was common throughout the country. The Trust was busily suing all independent manufacturers of films for patent violations (thereby hampering overall film production) but, was by itself or with its licensees, unable to produce anywhere near the volume of subjects required by an expanding market. Foreign companies, particularly Pathé Fréres, the world's largest producer of moving pictures, gladly filled the gap. In 1907, Pathé Fréres did twice as much business in the United States as the leading domestic producer.[24]

Statistics gathered in 1907 and 1908 from random issues of *Moving Picture World* (which in every issue listed the latest releases of all producers) confirm the prevalence of foreign films. Figures from these issues show that the ratio in 1907 was approximately 2 to 1, with 138 domestic films listed as opposed to 262 foreign ones. In 1908, the random tally came to 191 domestic and 298 foreign films.[25] For the first fifteen years of film's existence, the great majority exhibited in the United States were produced in Europe, although after 1908 the ratio dropped. While European films might have seemed either exotic or "educational" to middle- class Americans, it is likely that many in the immigrant audience found them somewhat familiar, perhaps nostalgic, which thereby added to their significance for that audience. In 1910, one writer in Chicago noted that in the ghetto nickelodeons of that city Pathé pictures were popular because they told their stories without subtitles, "and besides, the foreign settings of many of the pictures seem more homelike to the people who go to see them.."[26]

The MMPC vs. the Independents

Independent theater owners were being forced to choose sides--either to align themselves with the powerful, legally legitimate Trust and its imperious moralistic policies, or go with the feisty, more economically competitive "independents" who were beginning to challenge the Trust's grip on the market.

Despite the formation of the Motion Picture Patents Company (MPPC) in 1908, its monopolistic position and the constant threat of lawsuits, there was no shortage of entrepreneurs who, tempted by the promise of great profits to be made in the rapidly growing industry, formed their own producing companies. In 1909, Carl Laemmle, fed up with the Trust and determined to maintain a supply of films for his exchange, the Laemmle Film Service, formed the Independent Motion Picture Company, better known as IMP. In 1912 Laemmle combined IMP with several other independent companies--among them Pat Powers' Picture Plays, Bison Life, Rex, Nestor, and Champion (most of which had been in operation since 1909)--and changed the name of the company to Universal.[27]

Laemmle initiated a series of advertisements in trade publications that lampooned the Trust and urging exhibitors not to be victimized by the Trust's policies. A typical full-page ad (usually written by Laemmle's assistant, Robert Cochrane, a former advertising man), rhapsodized about exhibitors' satisfaction with independent films, and stated

> Maybe it isn't very dignified to dance a joy jig in public like this, but who cares a doggone for dignity! If you are not using Independent Films, you're missing the biggest hits of your life and that's absolutely

the truth.... Read my advertisement. I intend to tell you the straight news of what's going on. Then when you get good and sick of what you are up against, deal with me and forget all about licenses. Have you paid two dollars to get your hair cut this week?[28]

Another ad asked

Why stop at 10 percent? If you exhibitors continue to stand for that rotten ten percent penalty imposed upon you every time you switch your business from one to another licensed exchange, what on earth is to prevent the exchanges from eventually raising it to twenty or thirty or forty percent?[29]

Given the legal monopoly enjoyed by the Trust, it is not too far-fetched to suggest that only the myopic, autocratic and unbending nature of the Trust's management saved the independents from extinction. For what were all the theaters to do, particularly the ones in ghetto areas who could not measure up to Trust standards? The owners of these dingy, but financially successful theaters were understandably reluctant to put themselves out of business. If they could not get their films from the Trust, they would get them somewhere else. Some exchange and theater owners, like William Fox, objected to the high costs of Trust rentals and services and resented being told by outsiders what sort of programs they had to show. Many years later, Laemmle recalled the effect of the Trust's demands on exhibitors:

Well, you know what that did to the little fellows. They all had to come in or die, and they were invited to come in under contracts it was impossible to live up to.[30]

The experience of the Orpheum Company (which owned eight theaters in Manhattan, Brooklyn and Long Island) typifies the plight of the exhibitor up against the policies of the Trust. In September 1908, the company had signed a forty-week contract with the Vitagraph Company, who was to provide films for the Orpheum chain. But when Vitagraph joined Edison and others to form the Trust, which would not rent films to "unlicensed" theaters, the Orpheum Company discovered that "it could not obtain films unless it paid a license fee of two dollars a week for each theater until May next, when another arrangement would be made." The company was forced to go to court, seeking an injunction restraining the Trust from interfering with the Vitagraph Company's prior agreement.[31]

While the Orpheum Company did eventually win its case, such high-handed behavior by the Trust no doubt caused exhibitors to listen a bit more carefully to the appeals of the independents.

Social Interaction and the Appropriation of the Nickelodeon as Social Space

There is no evidence that the immigrant audience set about, with any sense of purpose, to "take possession" of the neighborhood theater. There was little or no agency involved; the profits clearly went to the exhibitor. Yet, the data made it clear that, with or without intent on the part of the audience, its appropriation of the theater as social space is what may have actually happened--at least, to a certain extent.

There is ample evidence in contemporary accounts that these neighborhood theaters did indeed become "social centers" and functioned as parts of the social sphere. Through the interaction as "private people come together as a public," the audience could and did exhibit the characteristics of the public sphere by exchanging information, engaging in debate, and assisting each other in sorting out and making sense of the authority-produced films exhibited.[32]

Theorists such as Miriam Hansen have accepted the validity of the notion of early motion-picture exhibition as an extension of the public sphere as conceived by Jurgen Habermas.[33]   This interaction and use of social space by immigrant audiences was accomplished spontaneously and without the "permission" of theater owners who, dependent upon continuous turnover, had little to gain and much to lose in such a relationship. For example, sitting through two or three complete shows must have seemed *gemultlicht* to some patrons in Jewish neighborhoods, but that could not have been construed as good news to theater owners--who eventually contrived means for discouraging such abuses, i.e., the "late pass."

Early articles and news stories consistently comment upon the lower class nature of nickelodeon audiences and their ethnic diversity. In 1907, a joint report issued by members of various New York civic groups (such as the Woman's Municipal League and the People's Institute) noted that there were 200 moving-picture houses in Manhattan, and that the "audiences are composit in the highest degree," observing that Chinese, Italians and Jews, young and old, and whole families sit side by side. "Outside," the report stated, "the vice and hopelessness of the Bowery. But inside was the enthusiasm of an orderly 300 people."[34]

As nickelodeons were introduced to working-class and immigrant neighborhoods in cities throughout the country, they received the same warm welcome. One exhibitor, in Philadelphia, pointed out that the film producers (who were still aspiring to middle-class audiences)

> should remember that they owe their success, not to our millionaires, but to the working class. The poor who have not the money to go to the high-class theaters are the ones supplying the cash.[35]

One publication referred to the nickelodeon as "the theater of the poorly paid--the little playhouse of the masses," a place where people who would rarely venture from the confines of their ghetto are given some of "the knowledge acquired by foreign travel." The writer cites a conversation with a laborer who said he couldn't imagine what a battleship looked like until he saw the Maine in a moving picture. Another worker said he'd never been to Paris, but had seen so many moving pictures of the city that the French capitol now seemed familiar to him.

Less exotic, perhaps, but equally edifying were the sights of the ocean and shoreline to those who lived far inland, or "the wonders of mountain and prairie" to the residents of coast states.[36] How else could a ghettobound immigrant (or, for that matter, almost any other American) see the Wright Brother's new flying machine in actual flight? But in this sense, and for this purpose, the films themselves were inseparable from the settings in which they were shown. Titles, for example, were meaningless to those who could not read English. It was only natural that a somewhat more educated viewer would translate the titles for a neighbor or friend in the next seat.

Not only titles needed translation. Very often the actions themselves required explaining. The sight of an actor on screen reading a menu and ordering a meal, could be bewildering to someone who had never been in a restaurant. Knowledgeable members of the audience helped guide viewers through the vagaries and nuances of city life--or, simply, life in the New World. Communication among viewers was lively and intense. Questions concerning customs, manners and romance abounded. The humble storefront theaters and nickelodeons became nodes of the public sphere, in which members of the audience seized upon the particular images on screen so they could come to terms with the even more dizzying and confusing aspects of the real world around them.

This determination on the part of the working-class audience to learn all the nuances inscribed within the visual symbols on screen, as well as the interactive nature of this process, although rarely commented on by contemporary writers, was visible to those who were sensitive to such social phenomena. W. Stephen Bush, a writer and editor for *Moving Picture World* and sometimes free-lance lecturer, found "nothing more interesting than watching the faces and the actions of the audience...in what are called the poorer sections of the city." He noticed this in 1908:

> If you offer to explain the pictures you need have no fear of interruption. They will listen to you with such attention and intensity that I am sure Oscar Hammerstein would prefer them as patrons to that wonderful 'cream of society.'[37]

A few months later, Bush again described the voluntary and uncontrolled nature of this interaction.

> Take any dramatic or historic picture; in fact, almost any picture, barring the magic and comic subjects. Stand among the audience and what do you observe? As the story progresses, and even at its very beginning, those gifted with a little imagination and a power of speech will begin to comment, to talk more or less excitedly and try to explain and tell their friends and neighbors. This current of mental electricity will run up and down, wild, irregular, and uncontrollable.[38]

Noticing this need for clarification, the theaters that could afford it hired "talkers" or (adopting middle-class terminology) lecturers to explain things to the audience.[39]

One writer described the "old men and women who are grandparents and parents" in the audience.

> Here they learn English words that they dare not ask of the younger generation for fear of being laughed at. They are usually very simple words, but difficult for the timid tongue. This wrinkled group forms the neighbor-questioning brigade in those motion-picture houses where lecturers are not; and many a time its members withdraw into a sallow, toothless shell, hurt because the neighbor has suddenly developed an attack of deafness.[40]

Some theater managers attempted to achieve some degree of control in their theaters, at the same time providing a more accessible program for their audiences. One resident recalled there had been

> a firehouse on Clinton Street [Lower East Side] which they turned into a movie. That was the silent movies. Not only did they have the man playing the piano, but because people couldn't read, they had a man and a woman with megaphones who would read the titles. When the actor spoke, the man read to the audience, When the actress spoke, the woman would read.[41]

This, of course, was more than lecturing. This was acting, and often the lecturers in these situations would act out their lines as well as recite them. When traveling exhibitor Lyman Howe put on a show, he employed "well trained assistants, who render the dialogue behind the screen." A *Moving Picture World* editorial writer noted a "common remark among the audience that 'it is as good as a real play.' " The editorial suggested that the

> services of a lecturer or reader may be beyond the means of some, but it is a poor ensemble if there is not some attache of the show that is qualified to intelligently lead the lecture while the slides are being shown. [42]

Harry Levine, who had been a nickelodeon lecturer, described a typical immigrant trying to learn English:

> That's where we lecturers came in. The fellow isn't as quick as he'd like to be. Here and there he can pick out a letter, maybe a whole word, but not a whole sentence. We read it to him, and, what's more, we explain it to him. That kind of fellow comes again and again, and he learns, believe me. [43]

When Mr. Levine uttered the foregoing words in 1920, the kind of theater he recalled was well on its way to extinction. No longer would neighborhood theaters serve as education and social centers. A new type of theater for a different type of audience was replacing the nickelodeon.

Participation Lost

Film historians David Bordwell, Janet Staiger and Kristan Thompson have studied the rise of the narrative film and linked it to the recapturing of the middle class audience. Gomery has posited the developing sophistication of exhibition practices as the stimulus for middle-class acceptance of moving pictures. [44] From about 1908 on, both production and exhibition underwent rapid development that had profound effects upon working- and middle-class reception.

While the public welcomed narrative films, there were other reasons for their acceptance by the producers. It is no coincidence that the rise in narrative films occured during the early years of the nickelodeon boom. As demand for all films increased, producers were hard pressed to provide sufficient product. The weakness of scenic films and actualities was their dependence upon the existence of events worth photographing. As one magazine writer later noted, "the demand for plays being greater than the supply of floods and fires, picture people began making pictures in the studios."[45]   Allen notes that Thomas Armat, Edison's associate, anticipated this situation in 1901, when he wrote to Edison:

> The problem with the motion picture business is that as things are now business runs by spurts. If there happens to be a yacht race or the assassination of a president, there is a good run on films for a few months.[46]

Cameras and crews had to be transported to and set up wherever the event-- which was not always predictable--was taking place.   Armat complained that in between such events, film crews wasted time and money "experimenting with costly subjects that the public will not buy."[47]   Story films, on the other hand, could be planned and scheduled in advance, and their costs could be controlled.   These factors meshed with the needs of exhibitors, many of whom changed programs every day and required a variety of fresh films on a regular basis.

The rise of the narrative film, and, perhaps more important, the improvements in film technique and content, probably would not have been sufficient to bring back the lost middle-class audience. Also required was segregation from the immigrant audience. Many of the exhibitors, as we have seen, were well aware of the social dynamics involved, and even while opening ghetto nickelodeons had been active in establishing higher class venues for well-mannered patrons who could afford the minimal twenty-five-cent price of admission. Both Fox and Loew had recognized the potential of this audience and had opened several relatively luxurious theaters as part of their individual "chains."   The Balaban & Katz organization in Chicago had strategically concentrated on "suburban" theaters of high quality for a middle-class audience. Balaban & Katz theaters offered clean rest rooms, free child care and, in 1917, the first air-conditioning.[48]

These theaters, usually featuring live acts among the moving pictures, were the forerunners of the spectacular, ornate movie palaces that would become almost common by 1920. Balaban & Katz determined that the presentation of films, not the films themselves, would be the key to success.   To depend exclusively on the drawing power of films would mean that their fate would rest in others' (the producers') hands, a prospect the partners found undesirable. Instead, Balaban & Katz built its chain of moving-picture theaters around five factors: the location of the theater, the theater building itself, service, stage shows, and air conditioning. These first moves toward the moving-picture palace had the dual virtue of being acceptable to the middle class while screening out the working class, much as vaudeville theaters had done. The large, ornate theaters charged at least a dime, and more typically fifteen or twenty-five cents. Here, middle-class patrons could relax among their own kind, free from the odors and antics of the lower classes.[49]

One critic, in 1909, described his visit to one such theater, the Atlantic Palace, on the Bowery.

> You pay your fifteen cents for a seat; you may smoke; waiters minister to your wishes for refreshments; you may move about; there is a gallery; and the entertainment is varied, vaudeville and equilibristic acts alternating with moving pictures... The pictures, however, constitute the major attraction...[50]

Eventually, the product became standardized to appeal to a mass audience; theaters became larger, capacities of several thousand being not unusual, segregation within the theater, by price of ticket, became possible and common. The cheapest seats, usually in the balcony, were occupied by the working class, while orchestra and box seats, which commanded higher prices, became the province of those who could afford them.

Certainly, as films grew longer, they became less usable for vaudeville houses. When moving pictures had been introduced as part of a vaudeville program, each film had been less than a minute in duration. Five- and even ten-minute films could fit nicely into a vaudeville house's schedule. But once films became longer than fifteen minutes--and even approached and sometimes exceeded half an hour, the nature of the vaudeville/moving-picture relationship changed. The houses that retained film eventually came to be seen as moving pictures with vaudeville, rather than the reverse.

Nickelodeons, too, found themselves unable to compete with the moving-picture palace, although it was not merely the latter's grandeur that did in the little theaters. By their nature and size, nickelodeons depended on a rapid turnover of the audience, and the increasingly longer narrative films had a drastic effect upon these theaters. As films became longer and more complex, rapid turnover became impossible. Further, producers began charging more for these longer films, but many nickelodeon owners were unable to charge more than a nickel or dime. In spite of slightly higher prices, even immigrant patrons would prefer the "fancier" theaters that were increasingly appearing on the outskirts of their neighborhoods. For the neighborhood nickelodeon or storefront theater, this trend meant their eventual extinction.

Where immigrants attended these more ambitious theaters, they found that a change in behavior was required: They could no longer assume they were among neighbors. Historian John Klasson has stated that vaudeville managers had "regarded overly demonstrative behavior, whether in approval or in disapproval, as bad for business." This description may be applied to the effect of the new movie theaters upon the working-class audience, who

> were caught in a dilemma. To continue to cheer, boo and call to one another...meant to stigmatize themselves as "uncivilized" boors unfit to associate with respectable families. [51]

Klasson noted that, for these audiences, "to behave themselves meant to accede to their own marginalization," and, for working-class audiences, that is precisely what happened. Jacobs claims that, as the poor became a less important segment of the audience, the themes that reflected their social reality grew fewer in number. (That assertion is questioned by some film historians, largely owing to the lack of supporting quantifiable data.) With the rise of the middle-class film audience, story lines mirroring leisure and luxury became dominant. To some degree, as Brownlow suggests, the rise of the "star system" may have helped retard the production of relevant socially critical films. Brownlow reasoned that, while it may have been acceptable for anonymous, unknown actors to play controversial roles-- such as dishonorable clergymen, unwed mothers or fallen women, such vehicles could hardly be expected of "stars," who had present and future reputations to protect.[52]

The new films themselves, with their strong story lines coupled with a style of performance that required attention to detail, in turn necessitated silent concentration. The change occurred over a period of years; where once they had enjoyed absolute freedom of behavior and used it to their advantage, immigrants increasingly found themselves bound by middle-class rules. Silence was demanded. Uniformed ushers patrolled the aisles, providing services and maintaining discipline. Working-class viewers were gaining luxurious surroundings and access to diegetic involvement, but in the process were losing their neighborhood social centers and any autonomy they may have possessed within the theater. Participants were becoming spectators.

6. DISCIPLINE AND ENTERTAINMENT

Architecture as Authority

While advances in narrative, editing and production were influential in modifying the behavior of audiences, the main conditioning site was the theater itself.

The Regent Theater, which opened in February 1913 on Seventh Avenue and 116th Street, is recognized as the first of the movie palaces.[1] According to historian Ben Hall, it was also New York City's "first deluxe theater built expressly for showing movies." It had been conceived as such by its owner, Henry N. Marvin, one of the founders of the Biograph Company.[2] Designed by Thomas W. Lamb and modeled after the Doge's Palace in Venice, it seated 1,800 . There was an eight-piece orchestra, a separate three-piece string ensemble, and the city's first movie pipe organ. The Regent's advertising referred to it as "The Cathedral of the Motion Picture."

Despite its good reviews, the Regent suffered diminishing attendance in the weeks and months that followed. A stock company of actors for a live dramatic interlude, was added to the program, but that didn't help. Movies were dropped altogether in June, and musical comedies were tried, without success. In desperation, Marvin turned to Samuel L.("Roxy") Rothapfel, who had built a reputation for taking over failing theaters, like the Lyric in Minneapolis, and the Alhambra in Milwaukee[3], and turning them into money-makers. His name is metonymic with the evolution of the movie palace.

Rothapfel, born in Stillwater, Minnesota, on July 9, 1882, was the "son of an immigrant German shoemaker and a Polish mother." When he was twelve, his family moved to New York's Lower East Side. Once there, Rothapfel was lost to the streets, holding a long series of menial jobs, none of which lasted more than a few weeks. By the time he was fourteen he had been banished from home by his father. A seven-year stint in the Marines was salutary, but when his enlistment ended it was back to unpromising, rootless jobs.

As an aspiring baseball player for a semiprofessional team in Pennsylvania, he picked-up the nickname "Roxy." It was easier to yell than "Rothapfel." He tried selling illustrated travel books in mining towns in Eastern Pennsylvania, with disappointing results. In 1907, on a sales trip in Forest City, Rothapfel stopped at a local tavern and was immediately taken by the tavern owner's daughter, Rosa. Then and there he gave up his sales career and talked his way into a job at the tavern. The owner, Julius Freedman, was delighted to have a well-traveled, articulate young man as bartender. Soon Rothapfel noticed a large room in the tavern, sometimes used for dances and party gatherings. It occurred to him that the room would be a good place to show moving pictures. He had seen them in the big cities; they were spreading everywhere. With Rosa's help, he persuaded Julius Freedman that movies were worth a try in Forest City.[4]

The Family Theater, as it was named, opened on January 1, 1908, using rented chairs and with a bed sheet serving as a screen. "The projector was a battered, hand-cranked Lubin's Marvel Cineograph." Admission was five cents. In addition to three reels of film, the audience was treated to a piano solo by Miss Mabel Rennie, a local pianist. The theater was a success! Managing it became a family enterprise when Rothapfel and Rosa were wed. He sought to enhance the movie-going experience, experimenting with lighting and offering classical solos by "my musical staff" between reels. Benjamin F. Keith, the owner of the Keith vaudeville theater chain had become aware of the Family Theater through its reputation as a crowd-pleaser, and he offered Rothapfel the job of improving the moving-picture exhibitions in his theaters. Rothapfel recognized this as a golden opportunity and quickly accepted.[5]

Now, in 1913, Rothapfel was being asked by Henry Marvin to rescue the ailing Regent theater. He studied the predominantly German-American neighborhood and correctly surmised that what this audience desired was a smattering of culture along with the entertainment. Rothapfel had the theater closed while renovations were made. To improve the picture, the projection booth was moved from the balcony to the orchestra floor. The size of the orchestra was doubled and placed on stage, just under the screen. Rothapfel saw to it that the music accompaniment matched the action on screen, a practice not yet employed in most theaters. A modern ventilation system minimized offensive odors and eliminated the need for the spraying of perfumed water, a common practice in many nickelodeons.[6] When the "new"

Regent opened in November 1913, W. Stephen Bush, a writer for *Moving Picture World*, was impressed. He praised Rothapfel for having created "a pleasant and agreeable atmosphere," and noted that

> there were things to delight the eye and ear before the entertainment proper had begun. A beautiful fountain played in front of the orchestra; the light effects had been most skillfully arranged; it was a happy medium between the glare and the somber.... For the first time in this country I was made aware of the possibilities of the music.

Bush also mentioned the quality of the image, in its sharpness and projected at "the right speed." Surrounded by such splendors, working-class patrons would most likely be inclined toward hushed restraint--no yelling across to a familiar face here! And the Regent *was* affordable, despite the fact that its evening admission was fifteen cents (except for box and loge seats, which were twenty-five cents). Although the latter were still out of reach, matinee prices were ten cents for all parts of the theater[7], an amount that was not unmanageable for segments of the working class in late 1913.

The middle class did not surrender easily. Avoidance of proximity to the working class was still desired. Bush, the most socially sensitive of the trade-paper writers, was mindful of the techniques employed to achieve this segregation:

> In many theaters, there are even at this day separate and less pretentious entrances to the gallery or second balcony, and while the distinctions may in some instances have been due to architectural necessity, it is a modern echo of the old belief that the poor must be herded and segregated in all fashionable places of amusement." [8]

Rothapfel went on to grander triumphs, rescuing the Strand on Broadway and 47th Street in 1914; the Rialto Theater, ("Temple of the Motion Picture") at Broadway and 42nd Street, in 1916; the Rivoli on Broadway and 49th Street in 1917; each palace being more splendid than its predecessor. Rothapfel's own fortunes had risen commensurately. He was earning approximately $600 a week.[9] The opening of the Strand was treated as a social event. Victor Watson, the drama critic of the *New York Times*, seemed to express many middle-class sentiments when he wrote:

> when I saw the wonderful audience last night in all its costly togs, the one thought that came to my mind was that if anyone had told me two years ago that the time would come when the finest looking people in town would be going to the biggest and newest theater on Broadway for the purpose of seeing motion pictures I would have sent them

down to visit my friend, Dr. Minas Gregory at Bellevue Hospital. The doctor runs the city's bughouse you know.[10]

Price policy assured class segregation: balcony seats were fifteen cents, loge or box seats cost fifty cents.

In 1926, Rothapfel rescued the ailing Capitol Theater on Broadway and 51st Street and reopened it as "The World's Largest, Coolest, Most Beautiful Theater," with no disagreement from reviewers. His crowning achievement was the theater he built for William Fox on Seventh Avenue and 51st Street in 1927--the Roxy, the "cathedral of the motion picture." Even by the standards of the day, the Roxy was exceptional. Its design signified the enthusiasm preceding the Great Depression. The theater's acoustics, ventilation and projected image were the finest money could buy. It was, as one report put it, the world's largest and greatest theater.[11]

Rothapfel's work represented one of several influences that had changed the texture of film presentation. An architect like Thomas W. Lamb was famous for his fantastic Persian oriental motifs, and his designs set the standard for two decades of motion-picture theaters. The contributions of these people, when they filtered down to the neighborhood "palace," inadvertently abetted the theater owner's desire for disciplined patrons. The surroundings were intimidating and somewhat awesome. Rude or boisterous behavior was obviously out of place. The uniformed ushers who patrolled the theater provided a "military" element.

A 1909 *Moving Picture World* editorial advised that "Most well-conducted moving picture houses have uniformed attendants," and recommended a company in Philadelphia that provided "special uniforms for moving picture theater attendants."[12]

Nor was the uniform seen by exhibitors as merely an embellishment--its value as a symbol of authority was well recognized. In 1910, one *Moving Picture World* writer, discussing attendants in movie theaters, noted that:

> We all respect the uniform because it is a mark of authority and order, whether the wearer be a policeman, soldier, sailor, clergyman or the like. We all need keeping in order, we all respect order, therefore we like order--or those of us who have properly regulated minds.... In recognizing the value of order they [theater managers] are taking the very proper and very obvious step of placing their attendants in uniform.... It pays because the public at large, as we have pointed out, recognize the value of order as symbolized by the uniform.[13]

That behavior control was not treated casually (and was worth a considerable investment) is implicit in a letter written in support of the foregoing viewpoint, which mentioned that in Boston's Theater Comique, "from its opening day its ushers, porters, doorkeepers and special policemen were uniformed. No moving picture [theater] has opened in that city whose employees were not uniformed."[14] More urgently, a series of articles in *Moving Picture World*, "The Modern Moving Picture Theater," in a chapter titled "Handling the Visitor," suggests the bouncer-like expectations regarding "ushers and attendants. The more vigorous these latter are in excluding undesirable visitors, the better for the reputation of the house." At some theaters there was even a "changing of the ushers" ceremony.[15]

The era of audience participation, during which the working class extracted direct social utility at its movie theaters, died over a period of years with scarcely a whimper. By 1920 nickelodeons were all but extinct. Larger, more ornate theaters predominated. Directors like D. W. Griffith, Erich von Stroheim and Cecil B. DeMille, stars like Charles Chaplin, Mary Pickford and Doug Fairbanks, films like *Birth of a Nation*, *Blind Husbands* and *Male and Female* had won over the middle class, and immigrant influence more truly represented its position as that of less than 18 percent of the country's population. In 1910, 14.5 percent of all United States residents had been foreign-born. Immigrants who had arrived between 1901-1910, during the second wave, constituted only 10 percent of the population.[16] For the years in question, that 10 or 15 percent signified more than 70 percent of the movie audience. Or, approached from another angle, 85 percent of the nation's population, attending all those high-priced vaudeville houses and middle class movie theaters, accounted for less than 30 percent of the movie audience.

Viewed historically, what immigrants, as the unheralded shapers of other people's destinies, were able to accomplish for the industry, keeping it alive and nurtured during a critical period, is impressive, perhaps even heroic despite its lack of planned effort, and at least worthy of recognition beyond that of merely "the audience." Social contributions by the working class are usually devalued and disregarded and that appears to be true in this instance. Had the immigrant audience not materialized, or had its response been similar to that of the middle class--initial fascination, then boredom, how would the industry have developed? What would have happened to Laemmle, Zukor or Fox? In 1910 Pathé was the world's largest film company and had been for many years. French-film historian Richard Abel contends that the nickelodeon would not have been able to develop without Pathé's presence in the American market.[17] Would Pathé have dominated American markets right up to the first World War, with strengthened production and distribution facilities in the United States, therefore changing the post-war dynamic? As it was,

World War I devastated European film companies, leaving the United States as the world's most powerful and productive source of moving pictures. Movies then became more popular than ever among all classes, but the lower class's brief moment of authority was over.

NOTES

Introduction

1. Harold Stadler, "The Spectacle of Theory," *Wide Angle*, vol. 8, no. 1 (1986), 4-5; Janet Staiger, *Interpreting Films* (Princeton: Princeton University Press, 1992), 11; Bruce Austin, *The Film Audience* (Metuchen: The Scarecrow Press, 1983), XIX.

2. Joyce E. Jesionowski, *Thinking in Pictures* (Berkeley: University of California Press, 1987), 1-2.

3. Eileen Bowser, *The Transformation of Cinema* (New York: Charles Scribner's Sons, 1990) 271, quoting an interview in MPW, 31 Jan 1914, 547-548. My own research (microfilm collection at the Library of Performing Arts, Lincoln Center, NY) failed to discover this interview, although a similar interview appears on page 531, but in a greatly abbreviated version. The only relevant phrase in this latter article is Dawley's observation that "One of the reasons why motion pictures have such popular appeal is because each individual follower of a scene is putting his own language into the mouth of the actor..."

4. C. David Mortenson, *Communication: The Study of Human Interaction* (New York: McGraw-Hill Book Company, 1972, 48-53; Pamela Shockley-Zalabak, *Fundamentals of Organizational Communications* (White Plains: Longman Publishing Group, 1991), 24-30.

5. John C. Merrill and Ralph L. Lowenstein, *Media Messages and Men: New Perspectives in Communication* (New York: David McKay Company, Inc., 1971), 33-45.0

6. Bernard Rosenberg, "Mass Culture Revisited," Bernard Goldberg and David Manning White, *Mass Culture Revisited* (New York: Van Nostrand Reinhold Company, 1971); 7, 6.

7. Ernest van den Haag, "A Dissent from the Consensual Society," Rosenberg and White, *Mass Culture Revisited*, 86; David Manning White, "Mass Culture in America: Another Point of View," Bernard Rosenberg and David Manning White, *Mass Culture* (Glencoe: The Free Press, 1957), 16.

8. Dwight Macdonald, "A Theory of Mass Culture," Rosenberg and White, *Mass Culture*, 59, 65; Herbert J. Gans, *Popular Culture and High Culture* (New York: Basic Books, Inc., Publishers, 1974), VII.

1. The Period of Introduction (1896-1905)

1. Neal Gabler, *An Empire of Their Own* (New York: Crown Publishers, Inc., 1982, 1.

2. Charles Musser, *Before the Nickelodeon* (Berkeley: University of California Press, 1991), 29.

3. Gordon Hendricks, *The Edison Motion Picture Myth* (Berkeley: University of California Press, 1961), 143, 144, 149-50.

4. Hendricks, *The Edison Motion Picture Myth*, 52, 171.

5. Musser, *Before the Nickelodeon*, 31.

6. Gerald Mast, *A Short History of the Movies*, 3rd ed. (Indianapolis: Bobbs-Merrill Company, 1981), 18, 19.

7. Joseph H. North, *The Early Development of the Motion Picture* (New York: Arno Press, 1973), 15; Musser, Before the Nickelodeon, 32.

8. *Scientific American*, 20 May 1893, 310.

9. Q. David Bowers, *Nickelodeon Theaters and Their Music* (Vestal, New York: The Vestal Press, Ltd., 1986), 2; Musser, *Before the Nickelodeon*, 42.

10. Terry Ramsaye, *A Million and One Nights* (New York: Simon and Schuster, 1954), 106-109.

11. Musser, *Before the Nickelodeon*, 45-47; Ramsaye, *A Million and One Nights*, 81.

12. Musser, *Before the Nickelodeon*, 47.

13. Ramsaye, *A Million and One Nights*, 212-215.

14. North, *Early Development of the Moving Picture*, 30-31.

15. Bowers, *Nickelodeon Theaters*, 5.

16. *This Fabulous Century*, 1900-1910 (New York: Time-Life Books, 1969), 9; Moses Rischin, *The Promised City* (New York: Corinth Books, 1964), 80.

17. Thomas Schlereth, *Victorian America* (New York: Harper Collins Publishers, 1991), 194. Photograph from Byron Collection, Museum of the City of New York.

18. Richard Koszarski, "Offscreen Spaces: Images of Early Screen Production and Exhibition," in Fell, Gong, Harris, Koszarski, etc., *Before Hollywood* (New York: Hudson Hills Press, 1987), 16; John Fell, "Cellulose Nitrate Roots: Popular Entertainment and Birth of Film Narrative," in Fell, Gong, Harris, Koszarski, etc., *Before Hollywood*, 39-40.

19. Musser, *Before the Nickelodeon*, 48.

20. Ibid., 57-59; Edward Wagenknecht, *The Movies in the Age of Innocence* (New York: Ballantine Books, 1971), 27; Ramsaye, *A Million and One Nights*, 119.

21. United States Government v The Motion Picture Patents Company, Equity No. 889, District Court, Eastern District of Pennsylvania, 1913-1914, 2068.

22. North, *Early Development of the Motion Picture*, 66.

23.Ibid., 37-39, 45, cites an ad in the London Times, 29 February 1896, 1D; Mast, *A Short History of the Movies*, 20.

24. Bowers, *Nickelodeon Theaters*, 4, 2; Mast, *A Short History of the Movies*, 18-20; North, *Early Development of the Motion Picture*, 28.

25. North, *Early Development of the Motion Picture*, 48-49.

26. Robert C. Allen, "The Movies in Vaudeville: Historical Context of the Movies as Popular Entertainment," in Tino Balio, ed., *The American Film Industry* (Madison: University of Wisconsin Press, 1985), 67.

27. Ramsaye, *A Million and One Nights*, 224.

28. Musser, *Before the Nickelodeon*, 60.

29. Ramsaye, *A Million and One Nights*, 236, Musser, *Before the Nickelodeon*, 62-63.

30. *The New York Dramatic Mirror*, Vol. 35, 2 May 1896, 19.

31. *New York Times*, 28 June 1896, 10.

32. Grau, Robert, *The Theater of Science*, (New York: Benjamin Blom, Inc., 1969), 9.

33. *New York Times*, 13 September 1896, "Notes of the Week," 18 B.

34. *New York Times*, 18 October 1896, "Notes of the Week," 11 B; Musser, *Before the Nickelodeon*, 91.

35. Bowers, *Nickelodeon Theaters*, 2; Musser, *Before the Nickelodeon*, 92.

36. Robert C. Allen, "Vaudeville and Film 1895-1915" (Ph. D. diss., University of Iowa, 1977), 5.

37. Will Irwin, *The House That Shadows Built* (Garden City: Doubleday Doran & Company, Inc., 1928), 80.

38. Ramsaye, *A Million and One Nights*, 232; *The New York Dramatic Mirror*, 2 May 1896, 19.

39. *The New York Dramatic Mirror*, "The Cinematographe at Keith's," 4 July 1896, 17.

40. *The New York Dramatic Mirror*, "Keith's Union Square," 11 July 1896, 17.

41. Henry Tyrrell, "Some Music Hall Moralities," *The Illustrated American*, Vol. 20, No. 335, 11 July 1896, 76, cited in George C. Pratt, *Spellbound in Darkness* (Greenwich, Connecticut: New York Graphic Society, Ltd.), 17.

42. Albert E, Smith, *Two Reels and A Crank* (Garden City: Doubleday & Company, Inc., 1952), 40.

43. *New York Telegram*, 15 October 1896, cited by Kemp Niver, *Biograph Bulletins*, 1896-1908 (Los Angeles: Locare research Group, 1971), 7.

44. Hillary Bell, New York Herald, 3 December 1899, cited by Garth Jowett, in Media Power and Social Control: The Motion Picture in America, 1894-1936, A Dissertation in History, Philadelphia, University of Pennsylvania, 1972, 36.

45. Upton Sinclair, *Upton Sinclair Presents William Fox* (Los Angeles: published by the author, 1933), 33.

46. Wagenknecht, *Movies in the Age of Innocence*, 15.

47. Ramsaye, *A Million and One Nights*, 240.

48. North, *Early Development of the Motion Picture*, 69, citing Frederick A. Talbot, *Moving Pictures* (1912), 135.

49. Smith, *Two Reels and A Crank*, 41.

50. *The Post Express*, Rochester, New York, 6 February 1897, 14, cited in Pratt, *Spellbound in Darkness*, 17, 18.

51. Bowers, *Nickelodeon Theaters*, 4.

52. Smith, *Two Reels and A Crank*, 47; Daniel J. Czitrom, *Media and theAmerican Mind* (Chapel Hill: University of North Carolina Press, 1982), 39.

53. Musser, *Before the Nickelodeon*, 480; Charles Musser, *The Emergence of Cinema* (New York: Charles Scribner's Sons, 1990), 303.

54. North, *Early Development of the Motion Picture*, 60.

55. *Moving Picture World*, 15 July 1916, 333.

56. *Moving Picture World*, cited in Bowers, *Nickelodeon Theaters*, 9.

57. North, *Early Development of the Motion Picture*, 61.

58. Ibid., 63, from *Ithaca Daily Journal*, 3 June 1897, 2.

59. Ibid., 63-65.

60. Ibid., *Early Development of the Motion Picture*, 73, citing *The Optical Magic Lantern Journal and Photographic Enlarger*, November 1894.

61. US v. MPPC, 1703.

62. *Literary Digest*, 18 December 1897, Vol. 15, No. 34, 1014.

63. Garth Jowett, "Media Power and Social Control ," dissertation, 1972, 45.

2. The Working Class: the Neglected Market

1. Thomas Sowell, *Ethnic America* (New York: Basic Books, Inc., Publishers, 1981), 77-78, 27-28; Loren Baritz, *The Good Life* (New York: Alfred A. Knopf, Inc., 1988) 15-16.

2. Stanley Feldstein and Lawrence Costello, eds., *The Ordeal of Assimilation* (New York: Anchor Press, 1974), 2-3.

3. John Bodnar, *The Transplanted* (Bloomington: Indiana University Press, 1985), 170-171, 23.

4. Ira Rosenwaike, *Population History of New York City* (Syracuse: Syracuse University Press, 1972), 83-84.

5. Baritz, *The Good Life*, 22.

6. John W. Briggs, *An Italian Passage* (New Haven: Yale University Press, 1978), 71.

7. Baritz, *The Good Life*, 27.

8. Moses Rischin, *The Promised City* (New York: Corinth Books, 1964), 10.

9. Michael Denning, "The Academic Left and the Rise of Cultural Studies," *Radical History Review*, 54, Fall 1992, 22, citing Daniel Bell, *The Reforming of General Education* (New York: Columbia University Press, 1960), 20.

10. Rischin, *The Promised City*, 9; Jacob Riis, *How the Other Half Lives*, (New York: Dover Publications, Inc., 1971), 19.

11. William Dean Howells, "Impressions and Experiences," quoted in Maurice Hindus, *The Old East Side* (Philadelphia: The Jewish Publication Society of America,

1969), 54; Irving Howe, *World of Our Fathers* (New York: Hartcourt, Brace, Jovanovich, 1976), 280.

12. Baritz, *The Good Life*, 23, 50.

13. Riis, *How the Other Half Lives*, 231, 6; Virginia Brainard Kunz, *The Germans in America* (Minneapolis: Lerner Publications Co., 1966), 19-20; Elizabeth Ewen, *Immigrant Women in the Land of Dollars* (New York: Monthly Review Press, 1985), 83.

14. Mary Antin, *The Promised Land* (Boston: Houghton Mifflin Company, 1969), 183-184.

15. Samuel Chotzinoff, *A Lost Paradise* (New York: Alfred A. Knopf, 1955), 68.

16. Ibid., 74.

17. Kathy Peiss, Cheap Amusements; *Working Women and Leisure Time* (Philadelphia: Temple University Press, 1986), 5.

18. Hutchins Hapgood, *The Spirit of the Ghetto* [1902] (Cambridge: The Belknap Press of Harvard University Press, 1967), 85.

19. Lawrence Bergreen, *As Thousands Cheer* (New York: Penguin Books, 1990), 10-11. Young "Izzy" was atypical. He grew up to be Irving Berlin.

20. Ewen, *Immigrant Women in the Land of Dollars*, 124, citing an article in *Survey 26* (1911), 69.

21. Ibid., 122, citing Elizabeth Watson, "Homework in the Tenements,' *Survey 32* (1914), 774.

22. Baritz, *The Good Life*, 48; Peiss, *Cheap Amusements*, 13.

23. Michael Davis, *The Exploitaton of Pleasure* (New York: Russell Sage Foundation, 1911), 3.

24. Chotzinoff, *A Lost Paradise*, 62.

25. James Huneker, *The New Cosmopolis* (New York: Charles Scribner's Sons, 1915), 5.

26. Margaret F. Byington, *Homestead: The Households of a Mill Town* (New York: Russell Sage Foundation, 1910), 4-5.

27. Ibid., 13-14, 23, 26, 36, 38.

28. Herbert G. Gutman, *Work, Culture ans Society in Industrialiizing America,* (New York: Alfred A. Knopf, Inc., 1976), 30.

29. Byington, *Homestead: The Households of a Mill Town,* 38.

30. Peiss, *Cheap Amusements*, 18-20.

31. Byington, Homestead: *The Households of a Mill Town*, 117. 112.

32. Peiss, *Cheap Amusements*, 22, 23.

33. Ibid., 34-35, 88-89.

34. Charles K. Turner, "The Daughters of the Poor," *McClure's*, November 1909, cited by Feldstein and Costello, in *The Ordeal of Assimilation*, 246-247.

35. Ewen, *Immigrant Women in the Land of Dollars*, 209.

36. Peiss, *Cheap Amusements*, 53.

37. Byington, *Homestead: The Households of a Mill Town*, 98.

38. Antin, *The Promised Land*, 272.

3. The Era of Participation (1906-1912)

1. Irwin, *The House That Shadows Built*, 103.

2. Douglas Gomery, *Shared Pleasures* (Madison: The University of Wisconsin Press, 1992), 16.

3. Charles Musser, *The Emergence of Cinema, the American Screen to 1907* (New York: Charles Scribner's Sons, 1990, 418-419; Kenneth Macgowan, *Behind the Screen* (New York: Dell Publishing Co., Inc., 1965), 124; Ramsaye, *A Million and One Nights*, 430; Bowers, *Nickelodeon Theaters*, 8, 28.

4. *The Billboard*, 15 October 1904, 34.

5. Musser, *The Emergence of Cinema*, 167.

6. Upton Sinclair, *Upton Sinclair Presents William Fox*, 35.

7. Miriam Cooper, Bonnie Herndon, *Dark Lady of the Silents* (Indianapolis: Bobbs-Merrill Company, Inc., 1973), 5.

8. Wagenknecht, *The Movies in the Age of Innocence*, 10.

9. "Moving pictures," *The Billboard*, 13 October 1906, 21; *Moving Picture World*, 13 July 1907, 297; *Harper's Weekly*, 24 August 1907, quoted in Bowser, *The Transformation of Cinema 1907-1915* (New York: Charles Scribner's Sons, 1990), 1.

10. *Moving Picture World*, 4 May 1907, 134.

11. Joseph Medill Patterson, *Saturday Evening Post*, 23 November 1907, 10-11.

12. Ibid., 10.

13. Michael Davis, *The Exploitation of Pleasure*, table 8, 30; Daniel J. Czitrom, *Media and the American Mind* (Chapel Hill: University of North Carolina Press, 1982), 48, citing Charles Stelzle, "How One Thousand Working Men Spent Their Spare Time," *Outlook 106*, 4 April 1914, 722-766.

14. *Moving Picture World*, 9 July 1910, 92.

15. *Moving Picture World*, 18 January 1908, 37.

16. Elizabeth Beardsley Butler, *Women and the Trades, Pittsburgh, 1907-08* (New York: New York Charities Publication Committee, 1909), 393.

17. *Moving Picture World*, 17 August 1907, 673.

18. *Moving Picture World*, 5 November 1910, 1043.

19. *Moving Picture World*, 4 July 1908, 7.

20. *Moving Picture World*, 22 August 1908, 139; Edward Armitage, interview by author, 12 June 1989, Hastings On Hudson, tape recording; *Moving Picture World*, 2 January 1909, 13.

21. *Moving Picture World*, 11 Janaury 1908, 22.

22. *New York Times*, 3 January 1909, pt. 5, 10.

23. "Origin and Growth of the Industry," a lecture by Adolph Zukor to Joseph Kennedy's Harvard symposium in 1927, reprinted in Kennedy (ed.), *The Story of the Films* (New York: A.W.Shaw Co., 1927), cited in Richard Dyer McCann, *The First Tycoons* (Metuchen: The Scarecrow Press, Inc., 1987), 81-82.

24. *Moving Picture World*, 20 June 1908, 528.

25. Robert C. Allen, "Motion Picture Exhibition in Manhattan," in John L. Fell, ed., *Film Before Griffith* (Berkeley: University of California Press, 1983), 165-167; Bowser, *The Transformation of Cinema*, 7; Ben Singer, "Manhattan Nickelodeons: New Data on Audiences and Exhibitors," *Cinema Journal 34*, No. 3, Spring, 1995, 5.

26. Walter Laidlaw, ed., *Statistical Sources for Demographic Studies of Greater New York, 1910* (New York: New York Federation of Churches, 1913), Map #154; E. Idell Ziesloft, in *The New Metropolis*, cited in Robert C. Allen, "Motion Picture Exhibition in Manhattan," in Fell, ed., *Film Before Griffith*, 167.

27. Ziesloft, *The New Metropolis*, cited by Allen in "Motion Picture Exhibition in Manhattan," in Fell, *Film Before Griffith*, 166-167. E. Idell Ziesloft, *The New Metropolis* (New York: D. Appelton and Co., 1899), 612, 635.

28. Grace Mayer, *Once Upon a City* (New York: The Macmillen Company, Inc., 1958), 138.

29. *Moving Picture World*, 16 January 1909, 70.

30. Allen, "Motion Picture Exhibition in Manhattan," in Fell, *Film Before Griffith*, 166.

31. Allen, "Vaudeville and Film 1895-1915", diss., 200, 213, 202, 212.

32. Montrose J. Moses, "Where They Play Shakespeare for Fice Cents," *Theater Magazine*, September 1908, 264.

33. Adolph Zukor, *The Public is Never Wrong* (New York: G.P. Putnam's Sons, 1953), 30-39.

34. Bosley Crowther, *The Lion's Share* (New York: E. P. Dutton, 1957), 23; Allen, "Motion Picture Exhibition in Manhattan," in Fell, *Film Before Griffith*, 173.

35. Norman Zierold, "The Film's Forgotten Man: William Fox," in McCann, *The First Tycoons*, 183-184; Siclair, *Upton Sinclair Presents William Fox*, 33-35; Musser, *The Emergence of Cinema*, 436.

36. Irwin, *The House That Shadows Built*, 273-274.

37. John Drinkwater, "The Trust Fight," in McCann, *The First Tycoons*, 49; Scott Berg, *Goldwyn* (New York: Alfred A. Knopf, Inc., 1989), 23; Ephraim Katz, *The Film Encyclopedia* (New York: Perigree, 19820, 677, 792, 1209.

38. Robert S. Sklar, *Movie-Made America* (New York: Random House, Inc., 1975), 41.

39. US v. MPPC, 1660.

40. *New York Times*, 7 March 1907, 2.

41. *Moving Picture World*, 4 May 1907, 220.

42. Robert M. Henderson, "Biograph," in McCann, *The First Tycoons*, 36.

43. *New York Times*, 18 December 1908, 3; *New York Times*, 19 December 1908, 4.

44. Bowers, *Nickelodeon Theaters*, 61; Balio, *The American Film Industry*, 25.

45. *New York Times*, 10 January 1909, 3.

46. *The Nickelodeon*, Vol. 1, No. 2, 1909, 39.

47. Ramsaye, *A Million and One Nights*, 427.

48. US v. MPPC, 1703.

49. Anthony Slide, *The American Film Industry* (New York: Limelight Editions, 1990), 136. .

50. *Moving Picture World*, 1 January 1909, 35.

51. Jowett, *Media Power and Social Control,* 52.

52. Peg Bosworth, interview by author, 14 June 1989, Hastings On Hudson, tape recording.

53. Frank LaMontagne, interview by author, 27 July 1988, Florence, Massachusetts, tape recording.

54. Judith Goldberg, *Laughter Through Tears--the Yiddish Theater* (East Brunswick: Fairleigh Dickinson University Press, 1983), 34.

55. Peiss, *Cheap Amusements*, 149.

56. *Moving Picture World*, 29 May 1909, 711.

57. Molly Hyman, in Jeff Kisselhoff, *You Must Remember This* (New York: Hartcourt Brace Jovanovich, 1989), 47.

58. Howe, *The World of Our Fathers*, 213.

59. Jacob A. Riis, "The People's Institute of New York," *Century Magazine*, no. 6, April 1910, 850; Russell Merritt, "Nickelodeon Theaters 1905-1914," in Balio, *American Film Industry*, 63.

60. Jane Addams, *The Spirit of Youth and the City Streets* (New York: Macmillan Company, 1910), 85-86.

61. *Moving Picture World*, 5 November 1910, 1043.

62. Simon N. Patten, in Czitrom, *Media and the American Mind*, 45.

63. Byington, *Homestead: The Households of a Mill Town*, 111.

64. Addams, *The Spirit of Youth and the City Streets*, 86.

65. *Moving Picture World*, 14 August 1909, 221; *Moving Picture World*, 19 March 1910, 417.

66. Frank LaMontagne interview.

67. Ruth Meacham, interview by author, 14 June 1989, Hastings On Hudson, tape recording.

68. Adelaide Jones, interview by author, Hastings On Hudson, tape recording.

69. Ruth Goldberg, interview by author, 13 June 1989, Hastings On Hudson, tape recording.

70. J. Hartnett, "Theater Managers Wake Up!," *Moving Picture World*, 15 May 1908, 525.

71. *Moving Picture World*, 4 March 1908, 203, quoting the Birmingham *Herald*.

72. Addams, *Spirit of Youth*, 86-87.

73. *Moving Picture World*, 29 June 1907, 262.

74. Kevin Brownlow, *Behind the Mask of Innocence* (New York: Alfred A. Knopf, inc., 1990), 5.

75. Nahma Sandrow, *Vagabond Stars: A World History of Yiddish Theater* (New York: Harper & Row, Publishers, 1977), 93.

76. Harry Roskolenko, *The Time That Was Then* (New York: The Dial Press, 1971), 149.

77. Edward Armitage interview.

78. Ruth Meacham interview.

79. Roskolenko, *The Time That Was Then*, 149-150.

80. *Moving Picture World*, 6 March 1909, 277.

81. Mary Heaton Vorse, "Some Picture Show Audiences," Outlook 98, 24 June 1911, 445; Peiss, *Cheap Amusements*, 152.

82. "Pictures Supersede Puppet Shows," *Moving Picture World*, 19 February 1910, 247.

83. Henry V. Hopwood, *Living Pictures*, London, 1899, cited in North, *The Early Development of the Motion Picture*, 74.

84. *Moving Picture World*, 22 February 1908, 143.

85. *Another Job for the Undertaker* , in "What Do Those Old Films Mean?," Noel Burch, videotape, Facets Video, Chicago, 1989.

86. Miriam Hansen, *Babel & Babylon* (Cambridge: Harvard University Press, 1910), 120.

87. Huneker, *The New Cosmopolis, 59*; Wagenknecht, *The Movies in the Age of Innocence*, 21; *Moving Picture World*, 15 February 1908, 116.

88. *Moving Picture World*, 26 October 1907, 541, citing an article in *The Manchester Evening Mirror*.

89. Ruth Goldberg interview.

90. *Moving Picture World*, 1 January 1909, 19.

91. *Moving Picture World*, 5 October 1907, 487.

92. *Moving Picture World*, 27 April 1907, 119.

93. *Moving Picture World*, 1 August 1908, 83.

94. *Moving Picture World*, 17 August 1907, 374.

95. See, for example, the films of the Corbett-Courtney fight (Museum of Modern Art Film Library or Eastman House archives), or photographs in *This Fabulous Century*, 1900-1910 (New York: Time-Life Books, 1969), 201, 272-273.

96. Hansen, *Babel & Babylon*, 119-120, 122.

4. Moving Pictures and Nickelodeons as Social Menaces

1. William Healy, "The Individual Delinquent," in Donald Ramsey Young, Motion Pictures--A Study in Social Legislation, University of Pennsylvania, Master's Thesis, 1922, 308.

2. *New York Times*, 2 May 1910, 5; *New York Times*, 27 January 1909, 7; "The Campaign to Curb the Moving Picture Evil in New York," *New York Times*, 2 July 1911, pt. 5, 15.

3. *New York Times*, "The Campaign to Curb the Moving Picture Evil in New York," 2 July 1911, pt. 5, 15.

4. Ibid.

5. Brownlow, *Behind the Mask of Innocence*, 4, 145.

6. *Moving Picture World*, 27 April 1907, 119.

7. Robert Fisher, "Film Censorship and Progressive Reform," *Journal of the Popular Film 4, 1975, 144.*

8. *Century Magazine*, April 1910, no. 6, 32.

9. Ewen, *Immigrant Women in the Land of Dollars*, 78.

10. *Moving Picture World*, 4 May 1907, 137.

11. *Moving Picture World*, 25 May 1907, 188; *Brooklyn Daily Eagle*, 2 June 1910, 118; *Moving Picture World*, 2 January 1909, 2.

12. *New York Times*, 3 January 1909, pt. 5, 10.

13. *Moving Picture World,* 9 January 1909, 32.

14. *Moving Picture World*, 4 March 1908, 203, quoting the Birmingham *Herald* .

15. *Moving Picture World*, 4 May 1907, 101, reprinted from the Chicago Tribune, 10 April 1907.

16. *Moving Picture World,* 1 June 1907, 198; World Book Encyclopedia, 1972, s.v. "Addams, Jane," "Hull House."

17. *Moving Picture World,* 1 June 1907, 198.

18. *Moving Picture World,* 29 June 1907, 262.

19. *New York Times,* 14 February 1909, 8.

20. *Optical Lantern and Cinematograph Journal,* December 1906, 50; *Moving Picture World,* 7 March 1908, 181; *Moving Picture World,* 25 April 1908, 369.

21. *Moving Picture World,* 9 October 1909, 483.

22. *New York Times,* 13 July 1910, 5.

23. *Moving Picture World,* 23 May 1908, 456.

24. Stephen Brier, Who Built America?, American Social History Project (New York: Pantheon Books, 1992), 126-129, 132-134.

25. *Moving Picture World,* 28 September 1907, 469.

26. *Torrington Evening Register,* 14 September 1907, 1.

27. *Torrington Evening Register,* 16 September 1907, 1.

28. Ibid.

29. Bess and Merrill Bailey, *The Growth Years* (Torrington: Torrington Historical Society, 1976), 40-43, 91-94, 97; John H. Thompson, *A History of Torrington* (Torrington: Torrington Printing Co., 1934), 33.

30. *Moving Picture World,* 15 May 1909, 634.

31. Ibid., 646.

32. *Moving Picture World,* 20 March 1909, 336.

33. *Moving Picture World,* 27 March 1909, 379.

34. *Moving Picture World,* 30 January 1909, 116-117.

35. Ruth Mezger, interview by author, 14 June 1989, Hastings On Hudson, tape recording.

36. Edwin McIntyre, interview by author, 14 June 1989, Hastings On Hudson, tape recording.

37. Kisseloff, *You Must Remember This,* 274.

38. Cooper, *Dark Lady of the Silents,* 5.

39. Gladys Cornwell, interview by author, 14 June 1989, Hastings On Hudson, tape recording.

40. Bowser, *The Transformation of Cinema,* 134.

41. Daniel J. Boorstin, ed., *We Americans* (Washington, D.C.: National Geographic Society, 1975), 352.

42. *Moving Picture World,* 23 September 1910, 698.

43. *Moving Picture World,* 16 May 1908, 433.

44. US v. MPPC, 1936.

45. *Moving Picture World,* 2 October 1909, 46.

46. Adelaide Jones interview.

47. *Ladies Home Journal,* January 1910, 32.

48. *Moving Picture World,* 4 January 1908, 5.

49. Frank LaMontagne interview.

50. "Seeing New York Through a Megaphone," "The Strange Girl in the Large City," *Ladies Home Journal,* January 1907, 17, 38; Henry Van Dyke, "Out of Doors in the Holy Land," *Ladies Home Journal,* November 1907, 9-10; *Ladies Home Journal,* January 1908, 5.

51. *Ladies Home Journal,* July 1909, 3.

52. Morris Rafael Cohen, "A Dreamer's Journey," quoted in Milton Hindus,*The Old East Side* (Philadelphia: The Jewish Publication Society of America, 1969), 47.

53. Quoted in Hindus, *The Old East Side,* 59.

54. Antin, *The Promised Land,* 270-271.

55. Ibid., 185.

56. Belle L. Mead, "The Social Pleasures of the East Side Jews," M.A. thesis, Columbia University, 1904, 13.

57. Lewis Palmer, "The World in Motion," Survey 22, 1909, 8-9, cited in Ewen, *Immigrant Women,* 88; Erik Erikson, *Childhood and Society* (New York: W.W. Norton & Company, Inc., 1963), 294.

58. Ida L. Hull, "Social Problems in Italian Families," National Conference of Social Work: Addresses and Proceedings 1929, quoted in Feldstein and Costello, *The Ordeal of Assimiliation*, 364.

59. Josephine Roche *The Italian Girl*, in Ruth S. True, "The Neglected Girl," West Side Studies (New York: 1914), 111, cited by Ewen, *Immigrant Women*, 106.

60. Maurice Hindus, *Green Worlds* (New York: Doubleday, Doran & Company, Inc., 1938), 217.

61. Harry Roskolenko, *When I Was Last On Cherry Street* (New York: Stein and Day Publishers, 1965), 6-7.

62. *Moving Picture World*, 31 December 1910, 1541; World Book Encyclopedia, Field Enterprises Educational Corporation, Chicago, 1972, Vol. 14, 157.

63. *Moving Picture World*, 2 November 1907, 557; Wagenknecht, *Movies in the Age of Innocence*, 14; *Moving Picture World*, 21 September 1907, 453; Musser, *The Emergence of Cinema*, 442.

64. *The Literary Digest*, 7 March 1908, 334.

65. Office of the Commissioner of Accounts, City of New York, "A Report on the Condition of Moving Picture Shows in New York," 22 March 1911, 4-14.

66. Ibid., 13.

67. *New York Times*, 26 March 1909, 2.

68. Ibid., 13.

69. Robert Anderson, "The Motion Picture Patents Company: A Reevaluation," in Balio, *The American Film Industry*, 143.

5 The Power of Metropolitan Nickelodeons

1. *Moving Picture World*, 23 September 1910, 698.

2. Ibid.

3. *Moving Picture World*, 10 September 1910, 570.

4. US v, MPPC, 323.

5. John M. Bradlet, "A Tour Amongst Country Exhibitors," *Moving Picture World*, 6 February 1909, 143.

6. *Moving Picture World*, 10 April 1909, 483.

7. *Moving Picture World*, 26 February 1910, 296.

8. US v. MPPC, 380.

9. Ibid., 380.

10. Ibid., 1832-1833.

11. *Moving Picture World*, 4 September 1909, 313; 28 August 1909, 287, 291.

12. Jack Warner, *My First Hundred Years in Hollywood* (New York: Random House, 1964), 61-62.

13. *Moving Picture World*, 28 August 1909, 277.

14. Ibid.

15. Musser, *The Emergence of Cinema*, 260; *New York Mail and Express*, 21 May 1898, 14.

16. Irvng Howe, *The World of Our Fathers* (New York: Hartcourt, Brace Jovanovich, 1976), 214.

17. Hansen, *Babel & Babylon*, 43.

18. *Moving Picture World*, 16 May 1908, 431.

19. Anthony Slide, *The American Film Industry* (New York: Limelight Editions, 1990), 50-51.

20. *The New Rochelle Pioneer*, 20 January 1906, pages unnumbered.

21. Ibid.: Richard Dyer McCann, *The First Tycoons* (Metuchen: The Scarecrow Press, Inc., 1987), 24, citing Grau, *The Theater of Science*, 1914.

22. *Moving Picture World*, 25 January 1908, 58.

23. *New York Times*, 9 February 1908, pt. 6, 1.

24. US v. MPPC, 1660.

25. *Moving Picture World*, 11 May 1907, 158; 2 November 1907, 569; 15 February 1908, 126; 25 July 1908, 74.

26. "Chicago Notes," *Moving Picture World*, 10 July 1910, 358.

27. Slide, *American Film Industry*, 365; Ramsey, *A Million and One Nights*, 495-496.

28. *Moving Picture World*, 15 May 1909, 618.

29. *Moving Picture World*, 8 January 1910, 3.

30. *New York Times*, 1 Dec 1912, pt. 5, 14.

31. *New York Times*, 19 February 1909, 16.

32. Jurgen Habermas, *The Structural Transformation of the Public Sphere* (Cambridge: MIT Press, 1991), 27.

33. Hansen, *Babel & Babylon*, 7-8, 13-16.

34. *Moving Picture World*, 22 February 1908, 137.

35. *Moving Picture World*, 10 October 1908, 282.

36. *Moving Picture World*, 24 August 1907, 392.

37. W. Stephen Bush, "Who Goes to the Moving Pictures?," *Moving Picture World*, 31 October 1908, 282.

38. W. Stephen Bush, "The Human Voice As A Factor In the Moving Picture Show," *Moving Picture World*, 23 January 1909, 86.

39. Bowser, *The Transformation of Cinema*, 18-19.

40. *New York Times*, 18 January 1920, pt. 4, 18.

41. Marty Cohen, born 1897, quoted in Kisseloff, *You Must Remember This*, 47.

42. "The Successful Exhibitor," *Moving Picture World*, 16 May 1909, 431.

43. *New York Times*, 18 January 1920, pt. 4, 18.

44. Bordwell, Staiger and Thompson, *The Classical Hollywood Cinema* (New York: Columbia University Press, 1985); Gomery, *Shared Pleasures*, 1992.

45. Harry C. Carr, "What's Next--2," *Photoplay*, March 1917, 60.

46. Thomas Armat, quoted by Allen, in "The Movies in Vaudeville," in Balio, *The American Film Industry*, 75.

47. Ibid.

48. Douglas Gomery, "U.S. Film Exhibition: The Formation of a Big Business," in Balio, *The American Film Industry*, 221-222.

49. Gomery, *Shared Pleasures*, 43, 31.

50. *Moving Picture World*, 27 February 1909, 235.

51. John F. Kasson, *Rudeness and Civility: Manners in Nineteenth Century America* (New York: Hill and Wang, 1990), 251.

52. Ibid.; Jacobs, *The Rise of the American Film*, 38; Brownlow, *Behind the Mask of Innocence*, xxi.

53. *Moving Picture World*, 19 March 1919, 417.

6. Discipline and Entertainment

1. *The Encyclopedia of New York City*, ed. Kenneth T. Jackson, Yale University Press, New Haven, 1995, 777.

2. *The Best Remaining Seats*, Ben M. Hall (New York: Clarkson N. Potter, Inc./Publisher, 1961), 31.

3. Hall, *The Best Remaining Seats*, 31, 29.

4. Ibid., 27-28.

5. Ibid., 28-29

6. Ibid., 32-33.

7. "The Theater of Realization," W. Stephen Bush, *Moving Picture World*, 15 Nov 1913, 714.

8. "The Triumph of the Gallery," W. Stephen Bush, *Moving Picture World*, 13 Dec 1913, 1256.

9. Hall, *The Best Remaining Seats*, 39, 45, 50, 53-54.

10. *New York Times*, 18 Jan 1914, pt. 4, 18.

11. Richard Koszarski, *An Evening's Entertainment* (New York: Charles Scribner's Sons, 1990), 23; Hall, *The Best Remaining Seats*, 66, 85.

12. *Moving Picture World*, 28 Aug 1909, 307.

13. *Moving Picture World*, 19 Mar 1910, 417.

14. *Moving Picture World*, 3 Dec 1910, 1293.

15. *Moving Picture World*, 9 Oct 1909, 482; Hall, *Best Remaining Seats*, 172.

16. "Immigration: The Demographic and Economic Facts," Washington, D.C.: Cato Institute and National Immigration Forum, 1995, 7-9.

17. Richard Abel, "'Pathe Goes to Town': French Films Create a Market for the Nickelodeon," *Cinema Journal,* 35, No. 1, 1995, 4.

BIBLIOGRAPHY

BOOKS

Addams, Jane. *The Spirit of Youth and the City Streets* . New York: Macmillan Company, 1910.

Allen, Robert C. "Vaudeville and Film 1895-1915." Ph. D. diss., University of Iowa, 1977.

American Social History Project. *Who Built America?* New York: Pantheon Books, 1992.

Mary Antin, Mary. *The Promised Land* . Boston: Houghton Mifflin Company, 1969.

Austin, Bruce. *The Film Audience* . Metuchen: The Scarecrow Press, 1983.

Bailey, Bess and Merrill. *The Growth Years* . Torrington: Torrington Historical Society, 1976.

Balio, Tino, ed., *The American Film Industry* . Madison: University of Wisconsin Press, 1985.

Baritz, Loren. *The Good Life* . New York: Alfred A. Knopf, Inc., 1988.

Bell, Daniel. *The Reforming of General Education* . New York: Columbia University Press, 1960.

Berg, Scott. *Goldwyn* . New York: Alfred A. Knopf, Inc., 1989.

Bergreen, Lawrence. *As Thousands Cheer* . New York: Penguin Books, 1990.

Bodnar, John. *The Transplanted* . Bloomington: Indiana University Press, 1985.

Boorstin, Daniel J. ed., *We Americans* . Washington, D.C.: National Geographic Society, 1975.

Bordwell, David, and Janet Staiger and Kristin Thompson. *The Classical Hollywood Cinema* . New York: Columbia University Press, 1985.

Bowers, David Q. *Nickelodeon Theaters and Their Music* . Vestal, New York: The Vestal Press, Ltd., 1986.

Bowser, Eileen. *The Transformation of Cinema* . New York: Charles Scribner's Sons, 1990.

Briggs, John W. *An Italian Passage* . New Haven: Yale University Press, 1978.

Brownlow, Kevin. *Behind the Mask of Innocence* (New York: Alfred A. Knopf, Inc., 1990.

Butler, Elizabeth Beardsley. *Women and the Trades, Pittsburgh, 1907-08* . New York: New York Charities Publication Committee, 1909.

Byington, Margaret F. *Homestead: The Households of a Mill Town* . New York: Russell Sage Foundation, 1910.

Chotzinoff, Samuel. *A Lost Paradise* . New York: Alfred A. Knopf, 1955.

Cooper, Miriam, and Bonnie Herndon. *Dark Lady of the Silents* . Indianapolis: Bobbs-Merrill Company, Inc., 1973.

Crowther, Bosley. *The Lion's Share* . New York: E. P. Dutton, 1957.

Czitrom, Daniel J. *Media and the American Mind* . Chapel Hill: University of North Carolina Press, 1982.

Davis, Michael. *The Exploitation of Pleasure* . New York: Russell Sage

Foundation, 1911.

Erikson, Erik. *Childhood and Society* . New York: W.W. Norton & Company, Inc., 1963.

Ewen, Elizabeth. *Immigrant Women in the Land of Dollars* . New York: Monthly Review Press, 1985.

Feldstein, Stanley and Lawrence Costello, eds. *The Ordeal of Assimilation* . New York: Anchor Press, 1974.

Fell, John L. ed., *Film Before Griffith* . Berkeley: University of California Press, 1983.

Gabler, Neal. *An Empire of Their Own* . New York: Crown Publishers, Inc., 1982.

Gans, Herbert. *Popular Culture and High Culture* . New York: Basic Books, Inc., Publishers, 1974.

Goldberg, Judith. *Laughter Through Tears--the Yiddish Theater* . East Brunswick: Fairleigh Dickinson University Press, 1983.

Gomery, Douglas. *Shared Pleasures* . Madison: The University of Wisconsin Press, 1992.

Grau. Robert. The Theater of Science. New York: Broadway Publishing Company, 1914.

Gutman, Herbert G. *Work, Culture and Society in Industrializing America,*. New York: Alfred A. Knopf, Inc., 1976.

Habermas, Jurgen. *The Structural Transformation of the Public Sphere.* Cambridge: MIT Press, 1991.

Hall, Ben M. *The Best Remaining Seats.* New York: Clarkson N. Potter, Inc./Publisher, 1961.

Hansen, Miriam. *Babel & Babylon* . Cambridge: Harvard University Press, 1910.

Hapgood, Hutchins. *The Spirit of the Ghetto* [1902]. Cambridge: The Belknap Press of Harvard University Press, 1967.

Hendricks, Gordon. *The Edison Motion Picture Myth* . Berkeley: University of California Press, 1961.

Hindus, Maurice. *Green Worlds* . New York: Doubleday, Doran & Company, Inc., 1938.

_____*The Old East Side* . Philadelphia: The Jewish Publication Society of America, 1969.

Howe, Irving. *World of Our Fathers* . New York: Hartcourt, Brace, Jovanovich, 1976.

Huneker, James. *The New Cosmopolis* . New York: Charles Scribner's Sons, 1915.

Irwin, Will. *The House That Shadows Built* . Garden City: Doubleday Doran & Company, Inc., 1928.

Jackson, Kenneth T. ed. *The Encyclopedia of New York City.* New Haven: Yale University Press, 1995.

Jesionowski, Joyce E. *Thinking in Pictures* . Berkeley: University of California Press, 1987.

Jowett, Garth. Media Power and Social Control: The Motion Picture in America, 1894-1936, A Dissertation in History, Philadelphia, University of Pennsylvania, 1972.

Kasson, John F. *Rudeness and Civility: Manners in Nineteenth Century America* . New York: Hill and Wang, 1990.

Katz, Ephraim. *The Film Encyclopedia* . New York: Perigee, 1982.

Kisselhoff, Jeff. *You Must Remember This* . New York: Hartcourt Brace Jovanovich, 1989.

Koszarski, Richard. *An Evening's Entertainment* . New York: Charles Scribner's Sons, 1990.

Kunz, Virginia Brainard. *The Germans in America* . Minneapolis: Lerner Publications Co., 1966.

Laidlaw, Walter. ed., *Statistical Sources for Demographic Studies of Greater New York, 1910.* New York: New York Federation of Churches, 1913.

Leyda, Jay, and Charles Musser, eds. *Before Hollywood* . New York: Hudson Hills Press, 1987.

McCann, Richard Dyer. *The First Tycoons*. Metuchen: The Scarecrow Press, Inc., 1987.

Macgowan, Kenneth. *Behind the Screen*. New York: Dell Publishing Co., Inc., 1965.

Mayer, Grace. *Once Upon a City*. New York: The Macmillen Company, Inc., 1958.

McCann, Richard Dyer. *The First Tycoons*. Metuchen: The Scarecrow Press, Inc., 1987.

Mast, Gerald. *A Short History of the Movies*, 3rd ed. Indianapolis: Bobbs-Merrill Company, 1981.

Mead, Belle L. "The Social Pleasures of the East Side Jews," M.A. thesis, Columbia University, 1904.

Merrill, John C. and Ralph L.Lowenstein. *Media Messages and Men: New Perspectives in Communication* . New York: David McKay Company, Inc., 1971.

Merritt, Russell. "Nickelodeon Theaters 1905-1914," in Balio, *American Film Industry:* 63.

Mortenson, C. David. *Communication: The Study of Human Interaction* . New York: McGraw-Hill Book Company, 1972.

Musser, Charles. *The Emergence of Cinema, the American Screen to 1907.* New York: Charles Scribner's Sons, 1990.

_____ *Before the Nickelodeon.* Berkeley: University of California Press, 1991.

Niver, Kemp. *Biograph Bulletins, 1896-1908.* Los Angeles: Locare Research Group, 1971.

North, Joseph H. *The Early Development of the Motion Picture.* New York: Arno Press, 1973.

Peiss, Kathy. *Cheap Amusements; Working Women and Leisure Time.* Philadelphia: Temple University Press, 1986.

Pratt, George C. *Spellbound in Darkness.* Greenwich, Connecticut: New York Graphic Society, Ltd.

Ramsaye, Terry. *A Million and One Nights.* New York: Simon and Schuster, 1954.

Riis, Jacob. *How the Other Half Lives.* New York: Dover Publications, Inc., 1971.

Rischin, Moses. *The Promised City.* New York: Corinth Books, 1964.

Rosenberg, Bernard and David Manning White. *Mass Culture.* Glencoe: The Free Press, 1957.

Rosenberg, Bernard, and David Manning White. *Mass Culture Revisited.* New York: Van Nostrand Reinhold Company, 1971.

Rosenwaike, Ira. *Population History of New York City.* Syracuse: Syracuse University Press, 1972.

Roskolenko, Harry. *When I Was Last On Cherry Street.* New York: Stein and Day Publishers, 1965.

_____ *The Time That Was Then.* New York: The Dial Press, 1971.

Sandrow, Nahma. *Vagabond Stars: A World History of Yiddish Theater.* New York: Harper & Row, Publishers, 1977.

Schlereth, Thomas. *Victrorian America.* New York: Harper Collins Publishers, 1991.

Shockley-Zalabak, Pamela. *Fundamentals of Organizational Communications* . White Plains: Longman Publishing Group, 1991.

Sinclair, Upton. *Upton Sinclair Presents William Fox.* Los Angeles: published by the author, 1933.

Sklar, Robert S. *Movie-Made America.* New York: Random House, Inc., 1975.

Slide, Anthony. *The American Film Industry.* New York: Limelight Editions, 1990.

Smith, Albert E. *Two Reels and A Crank* . Garden City: Doubleday & Company, Inc., 1952.

Sowell, Thomas. *Ethnic America* . New York: Basic Books, Inc., Publishers, 1981.

Staiger, Janet. *Interpreting Films*. Princeton: Princeton University Press, 1992.

This Fabulous Century, 1900-1910 . New York: Time-Life Books, 1969.

Thompson, John H. *A History of Torrington* . Torrington: Torrington Printing Co., 1934.

United States Government v The Motion Picture Patents Company, Equity No. 889, District Court, Eastern District of Pennsylvania, 1913-1914. Six volume transcript in Library of the Museum of Modern Art, New York.

Wagenknecht, Edward. *The Movies in the Age of Innocence* . New York: Ballantine Books, 1971.

Warner, Jack. *My First Hundred Years in Hollywood* . New York: Random House, 1964.

World Book Encyclopedia. Chicago: Field Enterprises Educational Corporation, 1972.

Ziesloft, E. Idell. *The New Metropolis* . New York: D. Appelton and Co., 1899.

Zukor, Adolph. *The Public is Never Wrong* . New York: G.P. Putnam's Sons, 1953.

ARTICLES

Abel, Richard. "'Pathe Goes to Town': French Films Create a Market for the Nickelodeon." *Cine Journal 35*, No. 1 Fall 1995: 4.

Allen, Robert C. "Motion Picture Exhibition in Manhattan," in Fell, *Film Before Griffith* , 1983: 165-167.

_____ "The Movies in Vaudeville: Historical Context of the Movies as Popular Entertainment," in Balio, *The American Film Industry* , 1985: 67.

Anderson, Robert. "The Motion Picture Patents Company: A Reevaluation," in Balio, *The American Film Industry:*, 1985: 143.

Bradlet, John M. "A Tour Amongst Country Exhibitors." *Moving Picture World*, 6 February 1909: 143.

Bush, W. Stephen. "Who Goes to the Moving Pictures?" *Moving Picture World*, 31 October 1908: 282.

_____ "The Human Voice As A Factor In the Moving Picture Show." *Moving Picture World*, 23 January 1909: 86.

_____ "The Theater of Realization." *Moving Picture World,* 15 Nov 1913: 714.

_____ "The Triumph of the Gallery." *Moving Picture World,* 13 Dec 1913: 1256.

"The Cinematographe at Keith's," *The New York Dramatic Mirror*, 4 July 1896: 17.

Carr, Harry C. "What's Next--2." *Photoplay*, March 1917: 60.

Denning, Michael. "The Academic Left and the Rise of Cultural Studies." *Radical History Review,* 54 (Fall 1992): 22.

Fell, John. "Cellulose Nitrate Roots: Popular Entertainment and Birth of Film Narrative," in Fell, Gong, Harris, Koszarski, etc., *Before Hollywood*, 1987: 39-40.

Fisher, Robert. "Film Censorship and Progressive Reform," *Journal of the*

Popular Film 4 (1975): 144.

Gomery, Douglas. "U.S. Film Exhibition: The Formation of a Big Business," in Balio, *The American Film Industry,* 1985: 221-222.

Hartnett, J. "Theater Managers Wake Up!." *Moving Picture World,* 15 May 1908: 525.

Hull, Ida L. "Social Problems in Italian Families," National Conference of Social Work: Addresses and Proceedings 1929.

"Keith's Union Square." *The New York Dramatic Mirror,* 11 July 1896: 17.

Koszarski, Richard. "Offscreen Spaces: Images of Early Screen Production and Exhibition," in Fell, Gong, Harris, Koszarski, etc., *Before Hollywood,* 1987: 16.

Macdonald, Dwight. "A Theory of Mass Culture," Rosenberg and White, *Mass Culture,* 1957: 59, 65.

Moses, Montrose J. "Where They Play Shakespeare for Five Cents," *Theater Magazine,* September 1908: 264.

Office of the Commissioner of Accounts, City of New York, "A Report on the Condition of Moving Picture Shows in New York," 22 March 1911: 4-14.

Palmer, Lewis. "The World in Motion." *Survey 22,* 1909: 8-9.

Patterson, Joseph Medill. *Saturday Evening Post,* 23 November 1907: 10-11.

"Pictures Supersede Puppet Shows." *Moving Picture World,* 19 February 1910: 247.

Riis, Jacob A. "The People's Institute of New York." *Century Magazine,* no. 6, April 1910: 850.

Rosenberg, Bernard. "Mass Culture Revisited," in Rosenberg and White, *Mass Culture Revisited,* 1971: 7, 6.

Singer, Ben. "Manhattan Nickelodeons: New Data on Audiences and Exhibitors," *Cinema Journal 34,* No. 3 (Spring, 1995): 5.

Stadler, Harold. "The Spectacle of Theory," *Wide Angle,* vol. 8, no. 1 (1986): 4-5.

Stelzle, Charles. "How One Thousand Working Men Spent Their Spare Time." *Outlook 106,* 4 April 1914: 722-766.

Tyrrell, Henry. "Some Music Hall Moralities," *The Illustrated American,* Vol. 20, No. 335, 11 July 1896: 76.

van den Haag, Ernest. "A Dissent from the Consensual Society," Rosenbeg and White, *Mass Culture Revisited,* 1971: 86.

Vorse, Mary Heaton. "Some Picture Show Audiences." Outlook 98, 24 June 1911: 445.

Watson, Elizabeth. "Homework in the Tenements." *Survey 32* (1914): 774.

White, David Manning. "Mass Culture in America: Another Point of View," Rosenberg and White, *Mass Culture,* 1957: 16.

Young, Donald Ramsey. "Motion Pictures--A Study in Social Legislation," University of Pennsylvania, Master's Thesis, 1922: 308.

SUBJECT AND NAME INDEX